MODERN MILITARY SERIES
Editor Michael Leitch

AIRCRAFT

by Christopher Chant
Introduction by Aram Bakshian, Jr

Octopus Books

First published in 1975 by Octopus Books Limited
59 Grosvenor Street, London W1
ISBN 0 7064 0427 0
© 1975 Octopus Books Limited
Produced by Mandarin Publishers Limited
22A Westlands Road, Quarry Bay, Hong Kong
Printed in Hong Kong

JACKET FRONT *The Harrier was the first operational V/STOL fixed wing strike fighter in the West.*
JACKET BACK *A Bf 110 being rearmed during World War II.*
PAGE 1 *A British RE8 being examined by her German captors in the spring of 1917.*
PREVIOUS PAGES *A converted Victor, formerly a long range nuclear bomber, refuels two Phantom fighters enabling them to greatly increase their operational range.*
THIS PAGE *One of America's latest fighters, the Grumman 'Tomcat' costing 'a competitive' eight million dollars each.*

Contents

Introduction

by Aram Bakshian, Jr.

Though dreams of conquering the heavens go back as far as recorded history, the conquest itself was a long time coming. Not so, however, was the conversion from peaceful to military uses once men and their machines had finally got off the ground.

Indeed, men's minds turned with remarkable haste to the idea of adding a further medium, the air, to those of land and water to make a third front in future wars. After a long period of faltering experiments with observation balloons that began at the close of the 18th century, the longed-for achievement of heavier-than-air flight at the start of the 20th century prompted rapid progress in the military domain. Soon, once-peaceful skies had developed into a major theatre of war—the decisive theatre, some would argue, in modern combat.

The debate on the relative significance of air power continues today. Scarcely a year passes without Parliament or Congress launching into fiery argument over the merits and demerits of new aircraft, while at the end of every military conflict (including the latest struggles in South East Asia and the Middle East) the rival advocates of land armies, manned aircraft and missiles re-fight on paper each campaign and in the process try to advance the cause of their most favoured arm.

Did the bombing of North Vietnam bring the Communists back to the peace-table or not? The debate still rages, as do others dating back to World War II: these concern such matters as the relative impact of the Luftwaffe on British morale during the Blitz, and the effectiveness of the Allied saturation bombing of Germany that followed. Vigorous partisans may be found to champion either side of such arguments.

One thing is certain. The most dramatic innovations in air warfare in the past few years have been in the missile field rather than in the continued refinement of piloted craft. In South East Asia the use of sophisticated ground-to-air anti-aircraft missiles took a gruelling toll of American bombers in the closing weeks of the war, and it was the development of a new 'self-aiming' bomb, rather than the introduction of new aircraft designs, that made American pinpoint bombing possible. Again, in the Arab-Israeli War of 1973 the crack Israeli Air Force was hit harder than ever before, not by Arab pilots but by Russian-built anti-aircraft missiles.

Yet no one seriously doubts the versatility and continuing usefulness of aircraft in wartime: for example, while the Israeli pilots in 1973 were paying a bloody price for air superiority, an American airlift to the Holy Land set new records for speed and efficiency in flying huge amounts of hardware and munitions to the distant battleground. This, joined to the superb fighting qualities of the Israeli Phantoms and their pilots, made a massive contribution to the outcome of the war.

The story of military aircraft is one of perpetual change, its turning-points depending in equal measure on courage in combat and ingenuity on the ground, where the concepts of aerial engineering, strategy and tactics are born. In this compact one-volume history, a valuable addition to the Modern Military Series published by Octopus Books, Christopher Chant tells us the exciting story in a concise narrative account amplified by a dazzling array of illustrations. From beginning to end it is good, informative reading and a solid foundation on which the serious student can base further research; while for the wargamer and the modeller there is an abundance of useful drawings, specifications and other helpful data.

OPPOSITE *A World War II German pilot's view of the Norwegian landscape, seen through the 'bubble' nose of a Heinkel He-111 medium bomber.*

Chapter One
The Early Days

For as long as man has dreamed of flying, there have been prophets of the purposes, both evil and good, to which the new art would be put. On the one hand there were men such as William Cowper (1731–1800), who wrote: 'I would . . . make it death for a man to be convicted of flying . . . Historians would load my memory with reproaches of phlegm, and stupidity, and oppression; but in the mean time, the world would go on quietly, and if it enjoyed less liberty, it would at least be more secure.'

On the other hand there were both practical and visionary men, among them Sir George Cayley (1773–1857), the pioneer of flying, and the poet Alfred, Lord Tennyson (1809–92). In 1816 Cayley wrote: 'An uninterrupted navigable ocean, that comes to the threshold of every man's door, ought not to be neglected as a source of human gratification and advantage.' Tennyson, though he feared that aerial warfare would be inevitable, was on the whole optimistic:

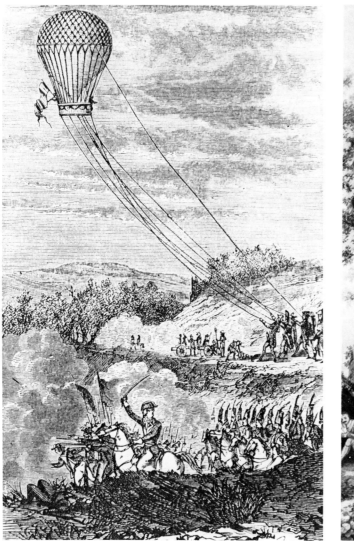

ABOVE *Sir George Cayley (1773-1857), many of whose designs anticipated the Wright brothers by almost a century.*
OPPOSITE *Military balloons in use as observation posts at the Battle of Fleurus, left, and the Siege of Mayence, both 1794.*
BELOW *Jacques Garnerin is shown making the first parachute descent from a balloon, in 1797.*

For I dipt into the future, far as human eye could see,
Saw the Vision of the world, and all the wonder that would be;
Saw the heavens fill with commerce, argosies of magic sails,
Pilots of the purple twilight, dropping down with costly bales . . .

(From *Locksley Hall*)

The warnings and exhortations of such men were, however, of little point until some means of flying had been invented. There had been many attempts to produce a flying machine since the days of Leonardo da Vinci (1452-1519), and a few even before his time, some laughable in their simplicity, others commendable for the courage they demanded of their authors. But they all fell foul of one particular obstacle: until the end of the 19th century, there was no power source capable of making the aeroplane a practical possibility. Men such as Cayley, quoted above, had investigated the problems of flight from the theoretical point of view and had produced flying machines that might conceivably have been capable of sustained flight had an engine been available; but this was not to be until the invention in 1885 of the first practical petrol engines, built independently by Karl Benz and Gottlieb Daimler.

Until then, the only successful aerial machines had been balloons. The first effective balloon was that invented by the Montgolfier brothers in France in 1783, its lift being provided from the hot air produced by a fire lit under the balloon.

The leaders of the French Revolution, which began in 1789, were avidly interested in any invention that might further their cause, and in the early years of the revolution set up a military balloon school. This institution had the honour of supplying the world with its first military airmen, whose observations from a balloon at the Battle of Fleurus in 1794 were instrumental in securing a French victory. Napoleon Bonaparte was not impressed by the potentialities of the balloon as a military weapon, however, and closed the balloon school.

Thereafter the balloon went into decline as a military vehicle for about the next fifty years. There were occasional attempts to revive interest in it, but the next time any use was made of balloons was in 1849, when the Austrians tried unsuccessfully to drop bombs from unmanned balloons on the besieged city of Venice. After a further pause the French once more turned to the use of balloons: in 1870, during the siege of Paris by the Prussians, several prominent Frenchmen and a considerable amount of mail were dispatched from the city by balloon.

Interest in military ballooning had also caught on in other countries. During the American Civil War of 1861-65 balloons were used sporadically by both sides to obtain information of the other's battlefield movements; but it was mainly the Unionist side, with its greater industrial capacity and inventiveness, that profited from the venture. The US Signal Corps established a balloon school in 1892 and attempts were made to use an observation balloon at the Battle

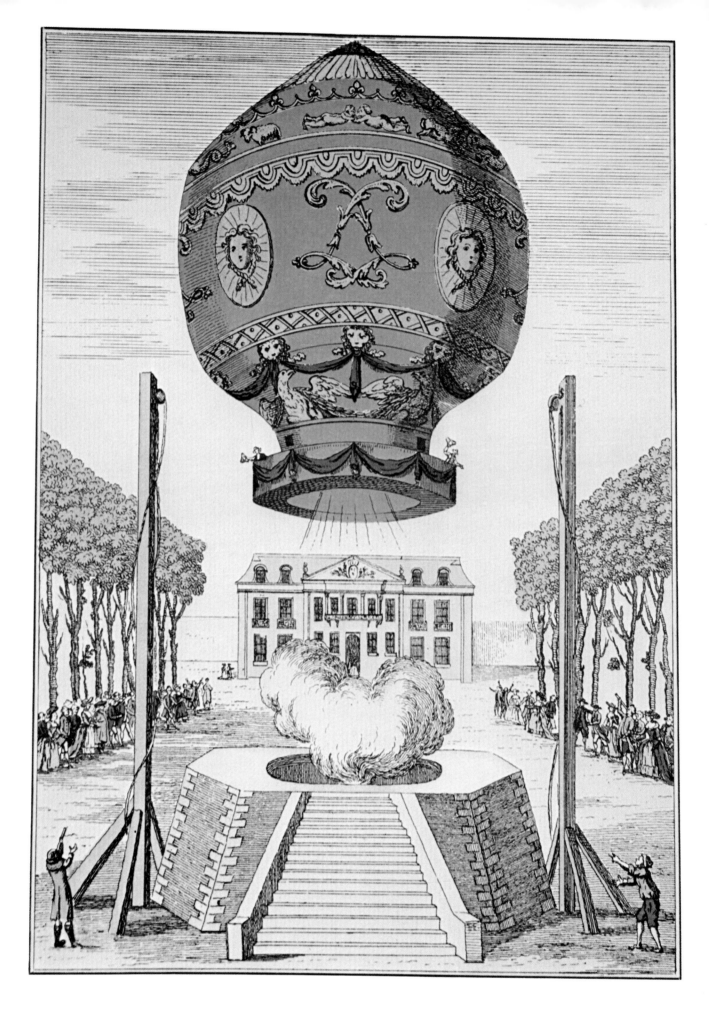

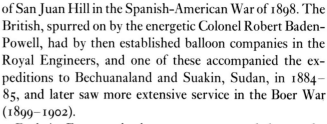

of San Juan Hill in the Spanish-American War of 1898. The British, spurred on by the energetic Colonel Robert Baden-Powell, had by then established balloon companies in the Royal Engineers, and one of these accompanied the expeditions to Bechuanaland and Suakin, Sudan, in 1884–85, and later saw more extensive service in the Boer War (1899–1902).

Back in Europe, the last component needed to make powered and sustained heavier-than-air flight a real possibility had by then been invented – the internal combustion engine. In its early forms, as developed independently by Benz and Daimler, the internal combustion engine was heavy, of low power and totally unreliable. But the basic idea was there, and design improvements swiftly followed. If the engine could next be coupled to some sort of lifting surface, the aeroplane would be ready to fly. In the meantime, other important developments had taken place.

As early as 1809 Sir George Cayley, the pioneer of aeronautics, had summed up the complexities of flight in a sentence: 'The whole problem is confined within these limits, *viz.* to make a surface support a given weight by the application of power to the resistance of air.' In other words, the

OPPOSITE *The hot-air balloon, designed by the Montgolfier brothers, in which Jean-Francois Pilâtre de Rozier, a 29-year-old French physician, made the first free (untethered) balloon flight by man, in November 1783; as crew he carried the Marquis d'Arlandes, who made an enthusiastic passenger but was none too keen on stoking the brazier to keep the balloon aloft.*
ABOVE LEFT *Inflating a balloon; from William Martin's* Parlour Book: or Familiar Conversations on Science and the Arts.
LEFT *A pioneer balloon in flight; from* Illustrations of Natural Philosophy, *published in 1850.*
ABOVE *A 'Montgolfiere' on the reverse of a medal struck to commemorate the work of the Montgolfier brothers.*

surface (the wings) must support the given weight (machine, pilot and load) by providing lift. This can only be done by making air flow round the airfoil section of the wing, normally by moving the wing forward through the air. In this forward motion the resistance of air (drag) must be overcome by the application of power (engine, or, in the days before sufficiently powerful engines had been developed, gravity). The first truly successful heavier-than-air craft, the gliders of Otto Lilienthal, depended on gravity for their motion because at the time (1891–96) the internal combustion engine was still not sufficiently developed to allow its use in a heavier-than-air craft.

But while heavier-than-air machines were still not possible, lighter-than-air craft had been able to profit by the invention of the petrol engine. Through a long and somewhat bizarre chain of experiments, the spherical balloon had been turned into an elongated cigar-shaped object, normally held in shape by an external beam, on which the pilot and the machine's cumbersome motor were located. This was the dirigible, an airship that could be flown in approximately the direction desired by the pilot if the weather were not too inclement. Power was still so low and controls so rudimentary that chance played a very important part in the progress of the early dirigibles. Among the pioneers in this field were the French-built versions of Santos-Dumont and Lebaudy.

In Germany, Count Ferdinand von Zeppelin had gone a stage further Rather than adapt the balloon, with all its attendant problems of maintaining the shape of the gas envelope, Zeppelin decided that the true future of the airship lay in a rigid framework containing gasbags for lift. Thus even if the pressure of the air fluctuated, or the gasbags

began to leak, the outside shape of the ship would not be altered and the engines could still propel it and the controls direct it along its course.

The development of a successful rigid airship was finally achieved by von Zeppelin in 1900 after considerable personal sacrifice, and the Zeppelin type of airship was later adopted by the German armed forces as a reconnaissance machine. Compared with early aircraft, it had excellent range, was relatively reliable and made a good observation platform.

The design philosophy of the Zeppelin was fixed virtually at the birth of the concept, and any improvements that were made were the result of better materials and more powerful engines, rather than of any radically improved design.

But while von Zeppelin was working with all his heart and resources on his airship designs, on the far side of the Atlantic the Wright brothers of Dayton, Ohio, were feeling their way carefully towards the world's first successful heavier-than-air, powered aircraft. Inspired and helped by Octave Chanute, doyen of American air enthusiasts, Orville and Wilbur Wright progressed from simple tethered gliders, on which they could check their control system, to free-flying gliders, and from there to their first powered machine, driven by an engine of their own design and construction. On 17 December 1903, at Kittyhawk, North Carolina, Orville Wright piloted the Flyer, as the brothers called their machine, for a flight of 12 seconds. It was the world's first powered, sustained and controlled heavier-than-air flight. Initial reports of the Wrights' success were greeted with scepticism, and the brothers worked on in obscurity for the next two years, perfecting what was in all ways a practical flying machine. This was the Flyer III, capable of reaching almost 40 mph and of staying in the air for nearly 40 minutes.

Realizing the importance of their invention, the Wrights on three occasions offered it to the United States Government, but each time they were rebuffed on the grounds that the Government had no interest in a machine that did not exist. This strange state of confusion had arisen partly because, shrewd businessmen that they were, the Wrights had not been prepared to let anyone see their creation until the patents covering it had been granted; and so the Government had thought that the brothers were asking for financial

aid to build the machine. Disgusted with the replies they had received from their own government, in 1905 the brothers then offered their machine to the British Government. But despite an enthusiastic letter from Colonel J.E. Capper, Superintendent of the Government Balloon Factory at Farnborough (which was later to become the Royal Aircraft Factory and the present Royal Aircraft Establishment), who had visited the Wrights and seen photographs of their machine flying, the British Government also turned

OPPOSITE, ABOVE *Otto Lilienthal flies one of the gliders which he developed in the 1890s and which were the first truly successful heavier-than-air craft. The next problem for the heavier-than-air school was to produce an engine that would give them powered flight.*

LEFT AND ABOVE *During the Siege of Paris in 1870 balloons were used to airlift men and mail by night to destinations beyond the Prussian lines. Many balloons fell short, however, and were captured. To remedy this a French engineer, Dupuy de Lôme, began developing a balloon with steering powers. With his first model he achieved a deviation of up to 22° from the direction of the wind; a propeller, turned by four men, drove the balloon up to 5 mph faster than the speed of the wind. Shown above is his Mark 2 model, driven by an eight-man propeller team.*

RIGHT *During the Boer War, the British 84th Battery and Balloon Corps are seen on the march towards Johannesburg. Balloons played a significant part in the observation work carried out in this war.*

BELOW *The* Luftschiff *in which Major von Parseval made slow but steady progress across the sky at the turn of the century; by this time the lighter-than-air balloon had exchanged its spherical shape for that of the cigar, and was termed a 'dirigible'. The tail fins served to keep the dirigible pointing into the wind.*
BOTTOM *In 1901 Alberto Santos-Dumont, a venturesome Brazilian living in France, made a startling aerial tour of the Eiffel Tower in a dirigible of his own design powered by a petrol engine. He made a round trip from St Cloud in under 30 minutes.*
OPPOSITE *The dream that was about to come true—powered and controlled heavier-than-air flight; this is an Avro Triplane.*

down their offer. The French Government, too, declined an opportunity to support them. Dejected by these rebuffs, the Wrights gave up all flying and experimentation for the next two years.

Although the general attitude shown towards the Wright brothers was one of scepticism, some informed members of the European aeronautical fraternity were prepared to give credence to the Americans' claims to have flown. The news in effect spurred the Europeans in their own attempts to produce a flying machine. There had already been numerous experiments, many of them initially encouraged by Lilienthal's successes, but the wonderful assortment of machines produced by Karl Jatho in Germany, by Robert Esnault-Pelterie, Ferdinand Ferber, Ernest Archdeacon and the Voisin brothers in France, by Samuel Cody and John Dunne in Great Britain, and by Jacob Ellehammer in Denmark were no more than tentative stepping stones – and not all of them in the right direction.

It was not until 12 November 1906, nearly three years after the Wrights' achievement at Kittyhawk, that the first European success was recorded. This took place when Alberto Santos-Dumont, a diminutive and dapper Brazilian

domiciled in France, made the first sustained flight in Europe in his 14-*bis*. Given that the machine was virtually a powered box-kite with no controls worth speaking of, this pioneering effort could hardly be called true, controlled flight; certainly the attempts to better Santos-Dumont's record (722 feet in 21 seconds) continued at a great rate.

Early in 1907, the 'pusher' biplane configuration (in which the engine is mounted behind the wing in order to 'push' the aircraft) was finalized in the Voisin-Delagrange biplane; but the aircraft itself was not successful when tested. That was in February and March, and it was not until 9 November that the first European flight of over a minute took place. On that occasion Henry Farman, an Englishman resident in France, flew a circular course of about 1,000 yards in his Voisin-Farman I pusher. At about the same time, too, Louis Blériot introduced the tractor monoplane layout to the world.

Prompted by the claims made by European aviators, the Wright brothers decided in 1908 to enter the lists once again. Wilbur Wright came to Europe, and Orville attempted once again to interest the US Government in the Flyer.

Wilbur Wright's visit to Europe proved devastating. His

complete and absolute mastery over his aircraft, not to mention the staggering performances he put up compared with his European rivals, astounded the European flying world. His best flights lasted for periods of around $2\frac{1}{2}$ hours, whereas the best of the European pilots had still to break the 30-minute barrier. Léon Delagrange put it perfectly: 'Well, we have been beaten. We just do not exist!'

Wilbur's astounding performances had the considerable benefit of encouraging European aviators to greater things. And here they had one distinct advantage – the rotary engine. This has a crankshaft fixed to the aircraft, and it is around this crankshaft that the cylinders revolve, with the propeller bolted to them. It was a particularly practical type of engine with an excellent power-to-weight ratio in comparison with its water-cooled inline counterparts. Moreover, the intense rivalry of the European aeronautical scene ensured that progress was kept going.

While Wilbur Wright was in France, Orville had been showing off the new Flyer A to the American military authorities at Fort Meyer near Washington. During the course of one of his demonstration flights, on 17 September 1908, the Flyer crashed and Orville's passenger, Lieutenant Thomas Selfridge, was killed – the first man to die in a powered aircraft accident.

The practitioners of early aviation were divided into two schools: those who believed that the aeroplane should be inherently stable and those who did not. The first school believed that the aeroplane should be all but capable of flying itself, so that the pilot was nothing more than a chauffeur, merely pointing the machine in the direction he wished to go. Most of the Europeans belonged to this school. The

LEFT *A free-flying glider built by the Wright brothers in 1901–02; from this they progressed to their first powered machine, which flew in 1903.*
TOP *Wilbur Wright photographed in a Wright Flyer in 1905.*
ABOVE *Wilbur Wright in 1903.*

other school believed that the relationship between pilot and aeroplane should be more in the nature of that between rider and horse, the two working together; it followed that the aeroplane should be unstable, so that the pilot had to fly it the whole time, and thus learn complete mastery of his craft. The chief adherents of this latter school were the Wrights. But with the increasing dominance in the flying world of European ideas, the chauffeur school prevailed. That it did so was to have considerable repercussions in World War I.

RIGHT *French pioneer Louis Blériot arrives at Dover after making the first-ever cross-Channel flight, on 25 July 1909.* BELOW *Henry Farman's No. 1* bis *pusher biplane; the engine is mounted behind the wing and 'pushes' the aircraft forward.*

Louis Blériot with his tractor monoplane; a front-mounted engine 'pulled' the aircraft.

The Antoinette Monobloc, a French-built design that favoured the monoplane layout and a more rigid wing structure than had formerly been used.

In those early days of flying, there were two ways of controlling the movement of aircraft in roll – by wing-warping and by ailerons. Given the flimsy structures then necessary for weight reasons, most early aviators favoured wing-warping, whereby lateral movement of the control column pulled wires which twisted the trailing edges of the wings up or down to deflect the airflow and cause the plane to roll. Others, notably Léon Levavasseur, favoured a more rigid wing with the outer rear portion of each hinged to a spar and moved by wires. This was first seen on the Antoinette IV in October 1908, and was accepted universally from about the middle of World War I.

The aeroplane was now a practical machine, and though performances were still low and gave little margin for error the more adventurous spirits turned their attentions to what could be done with the new machine in war. As it was still not capable of carrying much of a load, clearly the most important contribution it could make would be in the realm of reconnaissance, to keep the generals informed of what the enemy was doing. But the thought of doing merely this did not satisfy all those adventurous spirits. They foresaw a more active role for the new machine in war: attacking ships at sea, bombing railway junctions and even attacking the enemy's troops with machine-gun fire or small bombs. But the governments who would have to find the money, and the generals who would have to use them, were against aircraft being attached to their armies for any purpose other than as observation machines; even then the authorities were mostly sceptical of how useful aircraft might be. Since the end of World War I, much criticism has been levelled at these politicians and military men who were so loath to divert even a small amount of their armaments budgets to military aviation. But it should be pointed out in their favour that they were being asked to invest money in a new and completely untried weapon of war, one that even its adherents were compelled to admit was not reliable. Aircraft were still in their infant, experimental stages, and to standardize one type would have been foolish, whereas the supply problems caused by squadrons equipped with several different types could only provoke constant headaches. It is hard to see what else the European nations could have done, except perhaps to have laid better contingency plans for increased production in the event of the aeroplane finally proving itself.

Though depressed and bitter about what they considered to be military reactionism, air enthusiasts determined to go their own way and so demonstrate that the military were wrong. In the United States, Eugene Ely took off in his standard Curtiss biplane from an 83-foot platform built on the bows of the American cruiser *Birmingham* to be the first man ever to take off from a ship. That was on 14 November 1910. On 18 January 1911, Ely flew out to sea and landed on another cruiser, *Pennsylvania*, and then took off and returned to shore. Later that year, on 30 June, Glenn Curtiss

himself, the great designer-pilot, became the first man to carry out bombing runs when he attacked the buoyed outline of a battleship on Lake Keuka with dummy bombs.

Shortly after this, radio was used for the first time in an aeroplane: on 27 August the Canadian James McCurdy sent and received messages in his Curtiss biplane over New York State. Possibly the aeroplane's greatest contribution to the

Allied victory in World War I was made by artillery observation machines, and in this field radio was all-important. But the Horton set used by McCurdy was bulky, heavy and short-ranged, and much work had still to be done to make radio the practical possibility it later became.

Earlier in the year, on 26 January, Glenn Curtiss had introduced the world's first practical seaplane, and thus laid the foundations for the type of aeroplane that was to play so important a part in both world wars against the submarine.

In Germany, meanwhile, the Zeppelin had at last reached maturity, first as a passenger machine and then as a military one. This stimulated other, more slothful Europeans into thinking about what might happen in the event of another war, and the political leaders of what were to become the Allies began to take a more active interest in the aeroplane as a war-weapon, as witness the French *Concours Militaire* in October and November 1911 and the first substantial allocation of money for aircraft in Great Britain.

Several firsts in military flying have been mentioned above, and to these must be added the first live bomb test, made by a US Army Wright biplane in January 1911. This was also the year in which the machine gun first made its appearance in an aircraft, and though it is impossible to say who first took such a weapon aloft, the best mounting was that on the 1911 two-seater Nieuport.

The year 1912 was marked, in aeronautical circles, by the beginnings of a major military interest in aviation. Principally for military reasons of strength and reliability, a ban was somewhat abruptly imposed on monoplanes after a couple of accidents. This was a retrograde step, not least because no thorough investigation into the causes of the accidents was carried out. The effect of the ban was to hamper the development of monoplane aircraft in favour of structurally stronger biplanes built with trussed wing plan-

forms. Now, too, the pusher type was at last beginning to go out of fashion, to be replaced by the tractor biplane, which had a higher performance. The best example of this type to emerge in 1912 was the Royal Aircraft Factory's BS-1, designed by Geoffrey de Havilland. Another innovation of 1912 was the monocoque fuselage, which instead of having longerons braced internally in all three dimensions by wire,

OPPOSITE, ABOVE *Lieutenant Eugene Ely, the first man to take off from a ship (the USS* Birmingham*), here takes off from the US cruiser* Pennsylvania, *on which he had landed earlier the same day, 18 January 1911.*
OPPOSITE, BELOW *A Curtiss seaplane during naval manoeuvres off the Massachusetts coast.*
RIGHT *The Sopwith Batboat, a hybrid floatplane/flying boat type; the crew sat in the float-like hull.*
BELOW *The British Army Aeroplane No. 1, developed by Samuel Cody; by 1912 the military was showing a major interest in aviation, and in April of that year a Royal Flying Corps was established.*

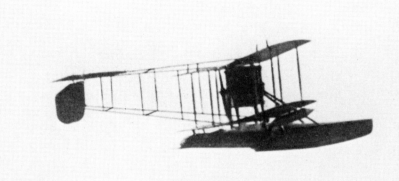

has an unbraced shell-like outer covering of wood or metal, which takes all the loads. The best example of this type of fuselage was in the Monocoque Deperdussin, which raised the world speed record to over 100 mph for the first time.

The growing importance of flying achieved almost universal recognition. In Great Britain, for example, a Royal Flying Corps was established in April 1912 and the first

Military Aeroplane Competition was held on Salisbury Plain in August that year. The Farnborough-designed BE-2, clearly the best aeroplane at the competition, was not allowed to compete because it had been designed at a government establishment. However, it flew *hors concours* and was judged the best machine present. Another step forward in British military aviation was the first successful

FAR LEFT AND ABOVE *A brace of Zeppelins, the rigid airships that the Germans were developing into sophisticated military machines; on the left is the Viktoria Luise, above another Zeppelin hovers outside its floating shed at Friedrichshaven.*
LEFT *The French-built Tubavion, an all-metal two-seat design.*
BELOW *The Monocoque Deperdussin; powered by a 160-hp Gnome engine, it was the first machine to exceed 120 mph.*

artillery spotting mission, flown by a BE-1 over Salisbury Plain. In France, too, the growth of the Zeppelin menace had led to the expansion of the national air force, particularly in terms of bombing aircraft; and in the massive manoeuvres, held in September near Poitou, aircraft were widely used. Finally, in this summary of events in 1912, the first parachute descent from an aircraft was made on 1 March in the USA by Captain Albert Berry.

The year 1913, the last full year before World War I, was a great one for flying. It will be remembered most of all as the year in which aerobatics was invented. The first man to loop the loop was a Russian, Lieutenant Nesterov, who did so on 20 August at Kiev. But the man who developed aerobatics more than any other was Adolphe Pégoud, a Frenchman. He perfected Nesterov's loop, and also many other manoeuvres, including inverted flight. All these seemed merely sensational at the time, but they were to be essential in the war that was looming ahead. While the French continued to break records (pushing the speed record up to 127 mph, the distance record to 635 miles and the altitude record to 20,079 feet), the British were beginning to produce the world's first true fighting planes: the Farnborough FE-2a fighter and the Vickers Destroyer. Other outstanding aircraft were also produced: the inherently stable BE-2, modified from de Havilland's design by T. E. Busk, and the Sopwith Tabloid, a small two-seater so manoeuvrable and

possessed of such a performance, especially in climbing, that the monoplane was more or less abandoned in Britain.

The other outstanding aeroplane of the year was the improved Deperdussin, which pushed up the speed record to 127 mph. This was also the year when the world's first four-engined aircraft appeared – the Russian Sikorsky Bolshoi, later developed as the huge Ilya Muromets bomber. The

the Libyan campaign immediately established the need for aerial photography, from which better maps could be made, and for air-to-ground radio so that artillery fire could be corrected. It also saw the first use of air-dropped bombs (4·4-pounders dropped by the pilot after he had pulled out the pin) and the first protest against bombing atrocities, by the Turks who claimed that a hospital had been hit.

Bolshoi, with a span of over 90 feet, could carry eight people for up to two hours – a phenomenal performance for the time.

Initially 1914 was a quiet year for aviation, and energies were devoted more to production than to innovation. The Ilya Muromets took the limelight from the Bolshoi when, on 11 February, it flew with 16 people on board; later it was ordered into production for the Imperial Russian Air Force.

This is an appropriate moment to look back to the first operations undertaken in war by aeroplanes. Contrary to general opinion, these did not take place in World War I but in the Turko-Italian War of 1911–12, when aircraft were used by the Italians in Libya. The Italian Army had received its first aircraft in 1910, and used them during the manoeuvres of August 1911. Here the four aeroplanes allocated to each army had proved entirely inadequate because of their low serviceability. The Italians were the first, in fact, to learn the lessons that Britain, France and Germany were to be taught the hard way in 1914 and 1915: above all they learnt of the need for a plentiful supply of reserve aircraft, for trained observers so that the pilot could concentrate on his flying, and for adequately trained ground crew.

The Italian Army also used small airships. These started operations in Libya together with a few aircraft on 23 October 1911, when Captain Piazza undertook a one-hour reconnaissance mission in a Blériot monoplane. The Italians were so short of aircraft that they eagerly welcomed the arrival of two flights of aeroplanes sent out by a Turin sporting magazine.

In terms of its influence on operations in World War I,

Had they troubled to do so, the military leaders of Great Britain, France and Germany could have learnt much more about air warfare from the Libyan campaign, particularly about the tactical reconnaissance operations that aircraft could be expected to undertake. Instead, their gaze was directed inward, their thoughts all too bound up with the holocaust that they were about to unleash on themselves.

OPPOSITE, LEFT *Dawn of the bomber; a Short Wright biplane of 1910 is shown, equipped with bomb release gear.*
OPPOSITE, RIGHT *A Sopwith Tabloid, a small and highly manoeuvrable two-seater introduced in the year before the war.*
BELOW *The giant Russian bomber Ilya Mouromets; in February 1914 this four-engined machine flew with 16 people on board.*
BOTTOM *The BE-2a, a staple aircraft in Britain's air strength in the period immediately before the outbreak of war.*

Air Warfare 1914-18
A Chronology

THE SYMBOL ☐ DENOTES ACTIVITY OVER A PERIOD OF TIME

1914

JUNE

28   Archduke Franz Ferdinand of Austria-Hungary assassinated at Sarajevo.

JULY

1   Naval wing of Royal Flying Corps becomes Royal Naval Air Service.

18   US Congress authorizes formation of Aviation Section in US Signal Corps.

28   Austria-Hungary declares war on Serbia.

AUGUST

1   Germany declares war on Russia, followed on 6th by Austria-Hungary.

3   Germany declares war on France and prepares to invade Belgium.

4   Britain declares was on Germany.

10   France declares war on Austria-Hungary.

11   RFC personnel start move to France.

12   Britain declares war on Austria-Hungary.

19   First RFC reconnaissance flight over France.

22   RFC reconnaisance detects Kluck's army moving against British Expeditionary Force.

23   Japan declares war on Germany.

25   First aerial victory: three machines of No. 2 Squadron down a German aircraft.

SEPTEMBER

5–10   First Battle of the Marne. Germans withdraw to a line Noyon-Verdun.

15–18   First Battle of the Aisne. Armies swing northwards to coast in the 'Race to the Sea'.

16   Formation of Canadian Aviation Corps.

OCTOBER–NOVEMBER

☐   Heavy fighting in Flanders. British Expeditionary Force denies Channel ports to German Army in First Battle of Ypres (30 October–24 November).

NOVEMBER

1   Allies declare war on Turkey.

DECEMBER

21   First air-raid on Britain.

☐   Germans dig in along Western Front, establishing static trench warfare from North Sea, near Nieuport, to Swiss border near Belfort.

1915

JANUARY

19–20   First Zepplin raid on Britain; bombs dropped on King's Lynn.

23   RFC reconnaissance detects Turkish forces moving towards Suez Canal.

FEBRUARY

15   First naval assault at Dardanelles.

18   Opening of first submarine campaign against Allied commerce.

MARCH

3   National Advisory Committee for Aeronautics established by US Congress.

MAY

2   Austro-German armies break through at Gorlice-Tarnow. Italy declares war war on Austria-Hungary.

31   First Zeppelin raid over London.

JUNE

7   Zeppelin destroyed in air by Flight Sub-Lieutenant R. A. J. Warneford.

AUGUST

12   Short seaplane makes first successful aerial torpedo attack, on Turkish merchantman in Dardanelles.

19   Colonel H. M. Trenchard takes command of RFC in France.

SEPTEMBER

14   Bulgaria declares war on Serbia.

15   Britain declares war on Bulgaria, followed on 16th by France.

1916

JANUARY

9   Evacuation of Gallipoli peninsula completed after disastrous eight-month campaign.

FEBRUARY

21   Battle of Verdun begins; air combats become increasingly common, notably Fokker Eindekkers against Nieuport Bébés.

MAY

17   Air Board formed in Britain to co-ordinate RFC and RNAS procurement.

JULY

1   Beginning of fighting in First Battle of the Somme; despite heavy casualties, RFC gains air superiority over the front and behind German lines.

AUGUST

27   Italy declares war on Germany; Rumania declares was on Austria-Hungary.

28   Germany declares war on Rumania, followed on 30th by Turkey and on 1 September by Bulgaria.

SEPTEMBER

2–3   First German airship brought down over Britain by Lieutenant W. Leafe Robinson.

15   Tanks make first appearance in final phase of Battle of the Somme.

OCTOBER

28   Death of Oswald Boelcke, father of true air fighting, in an accident.

NOVEMBER

28   First air-raid on London.

1917

FEBRUARY

1   Germans launch unrestricted submarine warfare against commerce.

FEBRUARY–APRIL

☐   Germans withdraw on Western Front to heavily defended zone—the Hindenburg Line.

MARCH

12   Start of the First Russian Revolution.

APRIL

6   USA declares war on Germany.

MAY

7   First night air-raid on London.

20   First U-boat (*U-26*) sunk by an aircraft (British flying boat).

25   First major daylight air-raid on Britain, by 21 Gothas.

JUNE

2   US Army's Signal Corps Aviation Section becomes Airplane Division.

13   First major Gotha raid on London kills 162 and wounds 426.

☐   First division of American Expeditionary Force shipped to France.

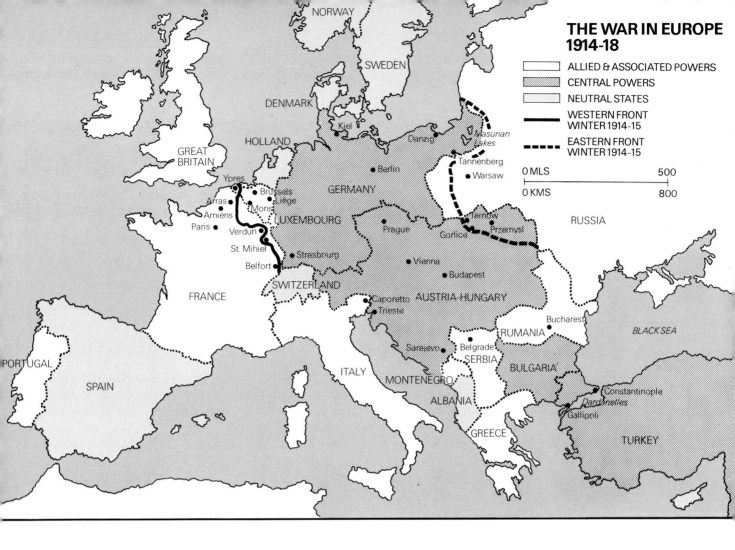

THE WAR IN EUROPE 1914-18

	ALLIED & ASSOCIATED POWERS
	CENTRAL POWERS
	NEUTRAL STATES
	WESTERN FRONT WINTER 1914-15
	EASTERN FRONT WINTER 1914-15

0 MLS   500
0 KMS   800

JULY

11   Cabinet committee set up to consider needs for air defence of Britain.

AUGUST

2   First successful deck landing, by a Sopwith Pup on HMS *Furious*.

22   Last daylight air-raid on Britain.

SEPTEMBER

2   First major night air-raid on Britain.

OCTOBER

11   RFC forms its 41st Wing, to bomb strategic targets in Germany.

NOVEMBER

7   Second Russian Revolution. Lenin and Trotsky sieze power.

DECEMBER

7   USA declares war on Austria-Hungary.

15   Russia and Germany agree armistice terms.

1918

JANUARY

2   Air Ministry formed in Britain.

MARCH

19   First operational sorties by American aircraft in France.

21   Ludendorff opens spring offensives on Western Front.

APRIL

1   Royal Air Force formed by amalgamating RFC and RNAS.

12   Last effective Zeppelin raid on Britain.

21   Death of Manfred von Richthofen, greatest ace of World War I with 80 victories, over the Somme.

MAY

19–20 Last effective air-raid on Britain.

JUNE

5   Formation of Independent Air Force under Major-General Trenchard for strategic bombing of Germany.

12   First bombing mission by US aircraft in France.

JULY

26   Death of Edward Mannock, greatest British ace of World War I with 73 victories, killed by fire from the ground.

AUGUST

8   'Black Day' of German Army; Allies advance seven miles in nine hours at Battle of Amiens.

28   John D. Ryan appointed US Assistant Secretary for War, with responsibility for Bureau of Aircraft Production and for Division of Military Aeronautics.

SEPTEMBER

5   Formation of Royal Canadian Naval Air Service.

12–16 American ground and combined air-ground assaults drive Germans out of St Mihiel salient.

OCTOBER

6   First German request for armistice.

14   Handley-Page bomber drops first giant (1,650-pound) bomb.

26   Major-General Trenchard becomes Commander-in-Chief of Inter-Allied Independent Air Force.

27   Ludendorff resigns. Austria-Hungary sues for armistice.

29   Mutiny at Kiel of German High Seas Fleet.

31   Revolution in Vienna and Budapest.

NOVEMBER

9   Revolution in Berlin.

10   Flight of the Kaiser.

11   Armistice concluded with Germany.

Chapter Two

World War I

World War I spread to most of the nations of Europe in the last days of July and the first days of August 1914. Few men at first saw how different this war was to be compared with earlier European wars, and the general consensus was that it would be a short, sharp war. Consequently, little or nothing had been done to prepare for a long conflict.

This is particularly evident in the use of 'air power' in the early months of the war. There were about 390 aircraft available to the combatants in the Western theatre of operations at the outbreak of hostilities (136 French, 48 British and 24 Belgian against about 180 German machines); but these were a hotch-potch of different designs that could hardly be grouped into homogeneous squadrons. The British were in the worst position, flying a motley of BE-2 variants, Avro 504s, Sopwith Tabloids and Bristol Scouts, plus a few French-designed machines. The French were slightly better off, being equipped with Morane-Saulniers of various types, Caudron G-IIIs, and a number of large Voisins which were pressed into service as rudimentary

bombers. The Germans were equipped with a large quantity of Taube types and Albatros B-Is and B-IIs. The Taube design had a large dove-like monoplane wing, and had been designed in Austria-Hungary by Igo Etrich. It was built in Germany by a variety of manufacturers in the early stages of the war.

With some notable exceptions, such as the Sopwith Tabloid and the Morane-Saulnier Type-N, most of these machines had a maximum speed of about 75 mph and an endurance of some three hours. Armament was officially forbidden by most authorities, and it was only the most enterprising of pilots who took a pistol or carbine with them. Moreover, as a result of the almost total lack of government preparation in the last years of peace, these aircraft were intrinsically civilian types and little able to undertake military tasks – the most important of which was to observe the enemy's movements. Thus, for example, in what was probably the best flying machine of all, the British BE-2b, the pilot sat in the rear cockpit while the observer found

OPPOSITE *A Bristol Scout, one of the British reconnaissance types in service at the beginning of the war.*
LEFT *The Avro 504, another British machine, here seen in peacetime colours. Best known today for its work as a trainer, the 504 was originally built in 1914 for reconnaissance and bombing work; its role was later extended to cover anti-airship and night-fighter duties.*
BELOW AND BOTTOM *The bird-like wings of the Etrich Taube (Dove), a reconnaissance machine designed in Austria-Hungary and built for widespread service by a variety of German manufacturers.*

himself in the forward one between the wings and surrounded by a mass of rigging wires, from which point he could achieve very little, so limited was his view. In the German Taube, the observer again sat in the forward cockpit, not this time surrounded by a Gordian knot of rigging wires, but right over the broad-chord wing, which again severely hampered his chances of making a successful reconnaissance.

The best types for reconnaissance in the early months of the war were the French Morane-Saulnier parasols and the pusher Farmans. The Morane-Saulnier Type-L clearly reflected that firm's design preferences: the wing was mounted above the fuselage on a framework of struts, supported by bracing wires. The crew, sitting underneath the wing, had an almost uninterrupted downward view. A different philosophy was apparent in such designs as the Farman MF-7 and 11. Here the design was based on the pusher principle, with the engine mounted behind the wings and driving a pusher propeller. The tail structure was

mounted on booms stretching back from the wings outside the disc swept by the propeller. Naturally enough, little in the way of slipstreaming could be achieved with such a design, and performance was lower than in tractor designs. But, more importantly perhaps in those early days, the crew was accommodated in a shoe-like nacelle perched on the leading edge of the wing. This afforded both the pilot and the observer an excellent view both forward and downward.

It was with such equipment that the airmen of World War I started their eventful careers; not surprisingly, the fear of mechanical failure on the part of their own aircraft was a far more dominant factor than any fear of enemy action. Even though many pilots ignored official policy and attempted to arm their aircraft, they were almost universally unsuccessful in providing themselves with effective armament. The first months of the war were marked by an amazing assortment of supposedly lethal gadgets fitted to aircraft: there were guns firing off at 45° to the line of flight in order to clear the propeller (which made sighting all but impossible); boxes of steel darts; some crews even carried grappling hooks or bricks fixed on the end of a length of line,

ABOVE *A rigging class held at the Crystal Palace for Probationary Flight Officers of the Royal Naval Air Service, introduced in July 1914. On the blackboard is a Farman biplane.*
OPPOSITE, ABOVE *A BE-2 stands outside the sheds; more than 3,200 BE-2s were built in several versions, and the type remained in active service until the Armistice.*
OPPOSITE, BELOW *A French Morane-Saulnier Type-L; its crew, seated underneath the wing, had an exceptionally clear view.*

with which they tried to break off enemy propellers. More important strategically were the French attempts to bomb German production centres in the south with their Breguets, and the Germans' efforts to use their Zeppelins over the Western Front. The Germans soon learnt, however, that small arms or light artillery fire was more than sufficient to cripple their very expensive airships: the target presented to the French gunners was large and, with all its hydrogen-filled gasbags, highly inflammable. Thereafter the Zeppelins were used for reconnaissance over the sea or over Russia, where the defences were not so strong, and for the bombing of England by night, when defensive fire would not be accurate.

The War on Land

Probably the most important single contribution made by aircraft in 1914 was the news brought by the crew of a British machine that the German right flank, which was intended to sweep round the west side of Paris early in September, had in fact veered more to the south and would now pass to the east of the French capital. This opened the eyes of the Allied High Command to the possibility of a counterstroke from Paris as the German flank moved past. The result was the Battle of the Marne, Germany's first serious setback in World War I, a setback that halted her victorious advance and set her hurrying back north in the 'Race to the Sea'. (This in turn gave rise to the continuous front and the stagnant war that produced such hideous casualty figures.)

As yet there were no true fighting aircraft. The machines described above were merely short-term expedients. The problem which held up further development is simple to describe: the machines with the highest performances, and therefore the best chance of catching an opponent and forcing him down, were the tractor-engined biplane scouts such as the Bristol Scout or Avro 504. But because they had a propeller in front of the pilot, it was impossible to mount a machine gun on the fuselage in such a way that it could fire forward through the disc swept by the propeller. Alternative measures were adopted, such as guns mounted to fire off at an angle from the line of flight, but they had little success.

A machine was then produced that can be considered as the world's first true fighting aeroplane. This was the Vickers FB-5, nicknamed the 'Gunbus', which had been designed from the outset for aerial combat on the guiding principle that if it was worth getting one's own air reconnaissance, it was also worth preventing the other side getting theirs. The Vickers FB-5 was a conventional two-seat pusher biplane, in which the pilot sat in the rear seat and the gunner/observer in the front seat, from which he commanded an excellent field of fire and observation. Armament was a single ·303-inch Lewis gun. This gun, which became one of the most successful aircraft guns of World War I, was an air-cooled light machine gun fed from a 47-round drum (later a 97-round drum was used). The chief fault of the FB-5 (the initials stood for Fighting Biplane) was that it was a pusher, with all that basic type's failings in terms of performance (speed 70 mph and ceiling 9,000 feet). The type began to arrive in France in February 1915.

The Vickers FB-5 was clearly not the answer. Fighting aircraft have always needed to have a higher performance than their quarry. The next step in the evolution of the fighter aeroplane was crucial but also, paradoxically, quite false. Early in 1914, Raymond Saulnier of the Morane-Saulnier company had seen where the true answer to air combat lay: this was in the production of an armament that fired along the line of sight and line of flight of pilot and

ABOVE *The Morane-Saulnier Type-N, a fast fighting scout capable of 102 mph at 6,500 feet; it served from 1914–16.*

BELOW *The Fokker Eindekker, first with the interrupter gear enabling the pilot to fire through the propeller.*

aeroplane. But the propeller of any tractor type would be in the way, so how was he to overcome this problem? Clearly it was necessary to halt the stream of bullets from the machine gun while one of the propeller blades was in the line of fire; this could be done, Saulnier saw, by synchronizing the action of the machine gun with the movement of the propeller. Saulnier designed an interrupter gear that would achieve this, but the uncertain quality of French machine-gun ammunition was such that rounds might 'hang fire' and then fire the bullet when the next blade was in the line of fire. To mitigate the effects of such stray rounds on the wooden propeller blade, Saulnier fitted wedge-shaped steel deflectors to the rear of each blade, along the line of fire. The problem of the ammunition appeared impossible however, and Saulnier abandoned his experiments. At much the same time as Saulnier was at work on the Allied side, a German designer, Franz Schneider, was conducting similar experiments with machine-gun interrupter gears for the LVG company.

In the spring of 1915, the French pre-war stunt pilot and aviation pioneer Roland Garros was serving with the French

PREVIOUS PAGES *An aerial dogfight, painted by N. C. Arnold.*
OPPOSITE, ABOVE *The Sopwith 1½-Strutter, a versatile machine that in wartime was a mainstay of the RNAS.*
OPPOSITE, BELOW *The Vickers FB-5 'Gunbus'; the observer/gunner, armed with a Lewis machine gun, sat in the front seat where he commanded an excellent field of fire.*
LEFT *The observer of an FE-2b demonstrates the manoeuvrability of his Lewis gun.*
BELOW *The Nieuport XI (Bébé), the fast and strong fighter that in 1916 began to restore Allied fortunes, shattered earlier in the 'Fokker scourge'.*

ABOVE *The pilot of a DH-2 single-seat pusher fighter is shown with his Lewis gun aimed along the aircraft's line of travel.*

Air Force. Disgruntled by his lack of success in shooting down German reconnaissance machines, Garros persuaded Saulnier to let him use the Type-L parasol monoplane fitted with the deflectors only, the interrupter gear having been removed. The results were startling. In less than three weeks Garros had disposed of five German reconnaissance machines. But then on 10 April he was forced down behind the German lines and captured, together with his machine.

The Germans at once realized the significance of the deflectors and decided to develop an efficient system for their own aircraft. A young Dutch designer working in Germany, Anthony-Fokker, was called in and told to produce a proper interrupter gear. Fokker promptly handed over all the information on Saulnier's device to his technical staff and told them to set to work. A few days later the result was ready for testing and proved entirely successful. Fokker persuaded the German authorities to allow him to test the new interrupter in one of his own aircraft, an M-5K monoplane, and, when the air tests proved equally successful, to order fighter aircraft using this device from him. The result was the Fokker E-I

ABOVE *A Bristol F-2B, the war's best two-seat fighter. Armed with one fixed, forward-firing Vickers machine gun and one or two free-firing Lewis guns, it entered service in 1917.*
RIGHT *In* Closing Up, *by G. Davis, the outgunned British pilots form a pack prior to breaking off contact with the enemy.*

monoplane, the world's first true single-seat fighter. In all ways an indifferent machine, indeed a dangerous one, the E-I nearly always prevailed by virtue of its superior armament – a synchronized 7·92-mm Parabellum machine gun. Later E-types had two or even three Spandau machine guns, though the fitting of three guns adversely affected the plane's performance.

In the hands of pilots such as Oswald Boelcke and Max Immelmann, the Fokker proved itself master of the skies over the Western Front, so much so that the period from autumn 1915 to spring 1916 is now known in aviation history as the time of the 'Fokker scourge', and machines such as the BE-2 as 'Fokker fodder'. The Allies had nothing to match the German fighter, and design work continued feverishly to find a counter.

Lacking an interrupter gear of their own, the French and British had to find other, short-term solutions while development went on. The first answer was the French Nieuport 11 or 'Bébé'. This was a compact, high-performance sesquiplane armed with a Lewis gun on the upper wing which fired over the propeller. (A sesquiplane is a biplane with the lower wing very much smaller in area than the upper wing.) Considerably faster, more manoeuvrable and stronger than the Fokker, the Nieuport 11 began the eclipse of the German type.

The Nieuport was soon joined in this task by Britain's answer, the Airco de Havilland (DH) 2. This was introduced in the spring of 1916 and was issued to No. 24 Squadron, which thus became the first British squadron to be equipped throughout with single-seat fighters. The DH-2 was a small pusher biplane with the Lewis gun mounted in the nose. The gun was at first movable, but most pilots found it better to fix the gun along the line of flight and aim the whole aircraft at the opposition. With the large-scale arrival of DH-2s in France the Fokker was totally outclassed and the Allies enjoyed a period of complete air supremacy. The other major fighting aeroplane of the day was the Royal Aircraft Factory's FE-2b, a big and sturdy two-seat pusher biplane that was used for escort, bombing and reconnaissance missions.

While the development of fighter aircraft had been progressing, the main burden of air operations rested on the shoulders of the crews of the various types of reconnaissance and artillery-spotting machines shuttling up and down the front. It was the protection or destruction of these all-important types that was the *raison d'être* of the new fighters. The requirements of their job made the recce planes large, stable and slow, and therefore difficult to defend against more nimble fighters.

The British were still using large numbers of the inherently stable BE-2s, but a new type, the RE-8, began to enter service in the second half of 1916. The RE-8 acquired an unenviable and not altogether justified reputation as a tricky aircraft to fly, but fulfilled its tasks excellently in the

The Germans, on the other hand, had decided early in the war that their reconnaissance aircraft should be more capable of defending themselves without a fighter escort than were the Allied machines. The result was a series of startlingly efficient biplanes. Albatros, a firm that was later to become famous for its shark-like fighters, introduced the C-III in 1916. This was not very fast (87 mph), but it had good range, adequate armament and it was very sturdy. The type was supplanted later in 1916 by the C-VII: this had a 200-hp instead of a 160-hp engine, which raised the top speed to 106 mph and made the aircraft much liked by its crews.

last two years of the war. It had a top speed of 102 mph, an endurance of $4\frac{1}{4}$ hours and an armament of one fixed ·303-inch Vickers machine gun, firing through the disc swept by the propeller with the aid of the newly developed British interrupter gear, and one (later two) Lewis guns for the observer. Another mainstay of the Royal Flying Corps and Royal Naval Air Service was the Sopwith $1\frac{1}{2}$-Strutter, a delightful machine to fly and one that was capable of fulfilling the fighter, bomber and reconnaissance roles. It was the first British aircraft to be designed with provision for an interrupter gear. Capable of 106 mph, it could climb to 15,000 feet, had an endurance of $4\frac{1}{2}$ hours and could carry up to 130 pounds of bombs.

In the French Air Force, reconnaissance was still carried out by the types that had been in service since the early days of the war – Farmans, Caudrons, and Morane-Saulnier Types LA and P. The last type was introduced in 1915 and had a speed of 97 mph, a ceiling of 12,000 feet, an endurance of $2\frac{1}{2}$ hours and an armament of one fixed Vickers machine gun and one flexible Lewis gun. These were by 1916 established as the main Allied machine guns.

The year 1917 saw the introduction of some of the best German reconnaissance machines of the war. Albatros developed the C-X and C-XII, strong and fast machines that were built in substantial numbers. In that year also came the widespread entry into service of the DFW C-V, developed late in 1916 from the earlier C-IV. The C-V was powered by the 200-hp Benz BzIV inline engine and had a top speed of 97 mph. With a ceiling of 16,400 feet and an endurance of $3\frac{1}{2}$ hours, it was one of Germany's best all-round aircraft, capable of undertaking reconnaissance, photographic, artillery-spotting and infantry contact-patrol work.

Infantry contact patrols were started in 1916 because commanders had been finding it impossible to establish where exactly their front-line troops had got to in offensives. Aircraft were thus sent out to find the markers which their troops had been ordered to lay out. The LVG C-V, designed by the same man as the DFW C-V, had a generally similar performance, and was one of the biggest two-seaters to see service with the Germans in World War I, having a span of 42 feet $7\frac{3}{4}$ inches. The Rumpler C-IV and C-VII both appeared in 1917 and did excellent work for the Germans. These were basically similar to other German reconnaissance types, but in addition they both had a very good high-altitude performance, which made them relatively immune from the attentions of Allied fighters.

In 1917, too, came the introduction of the best all-round aeroplane of the war, the Bristol F-2 Fighter. A very strong handy design, with the fuselage suspended between the wings, the Bristol Fighter had an inauspicious entry into service because its pilots tried to adopt normal two-seater defensive tactics. But once they recognized the machine's potential for offensive work, with the observer covering the

tail, the F-2A and its better development, the F-2B, became the war's best two-seater.

While this advance in two-seaters was taking place, the balance of air supremacy was again shifting to the Germans. The Allies had capped their defeat of the Fokker monoplane in early 1916 by introducing during the summer the Sopwith Pup fighter. This was essentially a single-seat scaled-down version of the $1\frac{1}{2}$-Strutter, and is generally recognized as the most perfect flying machine of World War I; with an engine of only 80-hp it was capable of 111 mph and had a ceiling of 17,500 feet, at which altitude it was still highly manoeuvrable. But armament remained unchanged at one Vickers machine gun. In the Allied squadrons the Pup was complemented by the Nieuport company's successor to the Bébé, the Nieuport 17. This had a single synchronized Vickers machine gun and a performance very similar to the Pup's, but with a 110-hp rotary engine. The rotary engine was now in its heyday, still being powerful enough to cope with the latest designs, but light and compact, thus giving the aeroplane extreme manoeuvrability.

OPPOSITE *The famous Sopwith Pup, a superb single-seat fighter capable of 111 mph on its 80-hp Le Rhône engine.*
TOP *The Albatros D-I, a powerful German fighter armed with two forward-firing Spandau machine guns at a time when most of its opponents carried only one gun.*
CENTRE *The French Spad S-7, a strong fighter that entered service in September 1916 with a 150-hp engine; one year later an improved model was introduced having a 175-hp engine.*
ABOVE *The Nieuport 17, the French successor to the Bébé and an Allied fighting partner of the Sopwith Pup.*

Royal Aircraft Factory SE-5a

The Scout Experimental (SE) 5a was the Royal Aircraft Factory's best design of the World War I period, and was bettered in results as a fighter only by the superlative Sopwith Camel. In design philosophy, the two standard fighters of the 1917–18 period were poles apart. The SE-5a (derived from the lower-powered SE-5) was a very robust, powerful machine, and enjoyed its combat success as a result of its speed, strength and stability as a gun platform rather than because of its agility.

The type was flown by most of Britain's top aces. As can be seen from the specifications, the SE-5a was powered by a variety of engines, the best of which was probably the Wolseley Viper. Deliveries of the SE-5a began in June 1917, and a total of 5,205 machines of the SE-5/5a family were built. Plans for the Curtiss company to build another 1,000 in the United States were cancelled after the war.

The SE-5a illustrated is fitted with a Wolseley Viper engine. Note the long exhaust (there was another on the port side) necessary to prevent the fumes adversely affecting the pilot.

The sturdiness of the SE-5a is immediately apparent from any photograph or illustration of the aircraft. To increase their aircraft's performance, No. 24 Squadron rigged their machines with reduced dihedral on the wings.

SPECIFICATIONS

Type		single-seat fighter
Engine		200-hp Hispano-Suiza, 220-hp Hispano-Suiza, 200-hp Wolseley W.4A Viper, 200-hp Wolseley Adder, or 200-hp Sunbeam Arab (all 8-cylinder liquid-cooled inlines)
Armament		one fixed, synchronized ·303-inch Vickers machine gun and one ·303-inch Lewis machine gun, plus four 25-pound Cooper bombs
Speed	126	mph at 10,000 feet
Climb	13	minutes 15 seconds to 10,000 feet
Ceiling	17,500	feet
Endurance	$2\frac{1}{4}$	hours
Weight	1,531	lbs (empty)
	2,048	lbs (loaded)
Span	26	feet 7·4 inches
Length	20	feet 11 inches
Height	9	feet 6 inches

Sopwith Camel

In terms of enemy aircraft destroyed (1,294), the Sopwith Camel was the most successful fighter of World War I, its only rival for the title of the best fighter of the war being the Fokker D-VII. Unlike the contemporary SE-5a, the Camel (developed from the Pup) was designed with extreme manoeuvrability in mind: the positioning of most of the heavy items of equipment (engine, fuel, guns, ammunition and pilot) in the front seven feet of the fuselage ensured this, although it took an experienced pilot to get the best out of the Camel. The F.1 Camel entered service in the middle of 1917, and was soon joined by a shipboard version, the 2F.1, which had a single Vickers gun and a Lewis gun on the top wing. A total of 5,490 Camels was built.

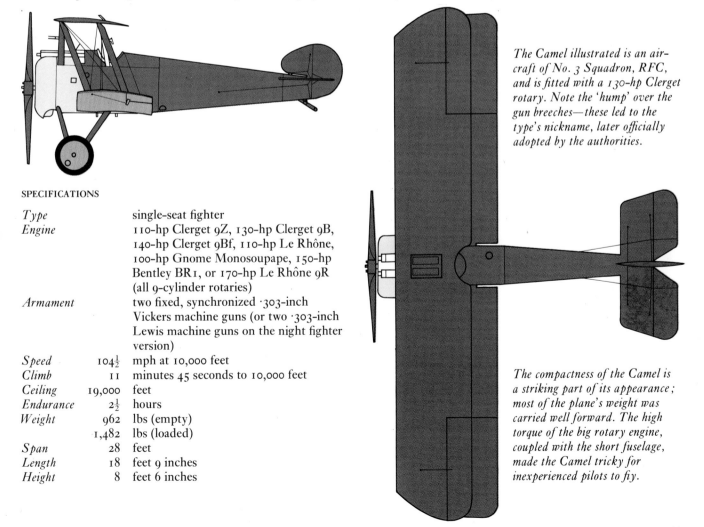

The Camel illustrated is an aircraft of No. 3 Squadron, RFC, and is fitted with a 130-hp Clerget rotary. Note the 'hump' over the gun breeches—these led to the type's nickname, later officially adopted by the authorities.

SPECIFICATIONS

Type		single-seat fighter
Engine		110-hp Clerget 9Z, 130-hp Clerget 9B, 140-hp Clerget 9Bf, 110-hp Le Rhône, 100-hp Gnome Monosoupape, 150-hp Bentley BR1, or 170-hp Le Rhône 9R (all 9-cylinder rotaries)
Armament		two fixed, synchronized ·303-inch Vickers machine guns (or two ·303-inch Lewis machine guns on the night fighter version)
Speed	104½	mph at 10,000 feet
Climb	11	minutes 45 seconds to 10,000 feet
Ceiling	19,000	feet
Endurance	2½	hours
Weight	962	lbs (empty)
	1,482	lbs (loaded)
Span	28	feet
Length	18	feet 9 inches
Height	8	feet 6 inches

The compactness of the Camel is a striking part of its appearance; most of the plane's weight was carried well forward. The high torque of the big rotary engine, coupled with the short fuselage, made the Camel tricky for inexperienced pilots to fly.

Of a different design philosophy was the French Spad S-7 fighter. This was a heavier and more powerful machine, still armed only with a single machine gun, but capable of 119 mph and a ceiling of 18,000 feet on the 175 hp of its Hispano-Suiza inline engine. Though lacking the rotary-engined fighters' agility and responsiveness, the Spad was immensely strong and an excellent gun platform. Deliveries began in August 1916.

The Germans, however, had gone a step further in the evolution of the fighter when they introduced the Albatros D-I and II fighters in the autumn and winter of 1916. Powered by a 160-hp Mercedes engine, the D-II had a speed of 109 mph at a ceiling of 17,060 feet. But whereas Allied fighters still had only one gun, the Albatros had two, which gave it a distinct advantage in firepower. The Germans followed up this advantage quickly, introducing the Albatros D-III in the spring of 1917. This was an updated D-II, with wings of greater span supported by V-shaped interplane struts instead of the earlier models' parallel struts. With the arrival of the D-III German

FOKKER TRIPLANE.

supremacy was complete, and the immediate result was 'Bloody April' 1917 – when Allied types, mostly British, were shot down in droves.

German supremacy did not last long, however. In spring 1917 the first of the Royal Aircraft Factory's new fighter, the SE-5, arrived in France, followed in early summer by its up-engined development, the SE-5a. The latter was powered by a 200-hp Wolseley Viper engine in its definitive version, compared with the SE5's 150-hp Hispano-Suiza. Both were armed with a synchronized Vickers machine gun in the fuselage and a Lewis gun firing over the propeller arc on the upper wing. The SE-5a had a top speed of 138 mph and a ceiling of 19,500 feet, with an excellent rate of climb as well, but like the Spad its chief qualities lay in its ruggedness and steadiness as a gun platform. The SE-5a more than held its own against all German fighters to the end of the war.

At about the same time that the first SE-5a's were reaching the squadrons, another new British fighter was making its appearance. This was the redoubtable Sopwith F-1 Camel, the war's most successful fighter (in terms of aircraft destroyed). The Camel was designed as a successor to the Pup. Although it had a slightly greater span than its predecessor, the Camel had a shorter fuselage. In the forward seven feet of this were crammed the pilot, fuel, guns and ammunition, and a 100- to 170-hp rotary engine. With most of the aeroplane's weight close to the centre of gravity, the Camel had phenomenal agility, though it took an experienced pilot to make the most of it. Moreover, its twin synchronized Vickers machine guns were a match for the twin Spandaus of the latest German fighters. With a 130-hp Clerget rotary, top speed was 115 mph and ceiling 19,000 feet.

Earlier in the year, in an effort to improve the pilot's view and increase the rate of climb – without losing any of the Pup's manoeuvrability – the Sopwith company had produced the Sopwith Triplane for the RNAS. This featured three narrow-chord staggered wings braced only by two plank-type interplane struts. The machine had a short and spectacular career until it was replaced by the Camel. Its most important contribution to the war in the air was to spark off a considerable number of German designs for triplane fighters.

Just as the Camel had succeeded the Pup, in the French Air Force the Spad S-13 succeeded the Spad S-7 in the early summer of 1917. Armed with two machine guns and equipped with a more powerful 235-hp Hispano-Suiza inline engine, the Spad S-13 also had aerodynamic refinements intended to improve manoeuvrability. Like the SE-5a, it had a top speed of 138 mph, but it had a better ceiling (21,800 feet) and proved capable of taking on the latest German fighters up to the end of the war.

Spurred on by these Allied successes, the Germans also continued to improve their fighters. The Albatros works produced another version of their basic fighter design in the summer of 1917. This was the D-V, powered by a 180-hp Mercedes inline. Basically similar to the D-III, the D-V was not much of an improvement on the earlier type, having a speed of 116 mph and a ceiling of 20,500 feet. Essentially, the problem was that the design had reached its development limit; what was needed was another design.

The first new design to be produced in any quantity was

OPPOSITE *Two Fokker types that made an impact in the latter stages of the war: the Dr-I triplane, an agile machine inspired by the Sopwith Triplane, and the excellent D-VII.*

ABOVE *The Sopwith Triplane, produced for the RNAS; the design was chosen because it improved on the Pup's rate of climb and manoeuvrability.*

the Fokker Dr-I. This was a diminutive triplane inspired by the Sopwith Triplane. It was slow (103 mph) compared with contemporary Allied designs, but its ceiling and rate of climb were good and its manoeuvrability excellent. In the hands of skilled pilots it performed usefully, but it was not the answer to Allied superiority.

The right answer was not in fact found until 1918, when the Fokker D-VII made its appearance. This design entered service in April 1918. It was powered by a 185-hp BMW inline engine and had a top speed of 124 mph and a ceiling of 22,900 feet. But though its performance was only about the same as that of Allied fighters, its handling qualities at altitude, and its ability to 'hang' on its propeller, made it a formidable fighter. Fokker's last fighter of the war, the D-VIII, is also worthy of note. This was a parasol-winged machine, powered by a rotary and not very fast, but agile with good rates of climb and dive. Only a few were completed before the end of the war.

In the Allied camp, a new generation of fighters would have entered the lists in large numbers if the war had continued into 1919, and some of these should be mentioned.

Sopwith had just introduced two good designs, the Snipe fighter, a faster development of the Camel, and the Dolphin escort and ground-attack fighter. Another manufacturer, Martin & Handasyde, was about to commence large-scale delivery of the fastest Allied fighter to appear during the war, the F-4 Buzzard, which was powered by a 300-hp Hispano-Suiza inline and had a top speed of 145 mph. The French were about to introduce the latest of the Nieuport line, which was the first of that company's fighters not to be powered with an inline engine. This was the Nieuport 29, a lumpy and not very attractive design that was nevertheless fast and rugged.

Although the fighters were best-known to the public, and made the greatest advances in performance, there were other types of aircraft operating over the front that proved the real work-horses of the war. Whereas the early years from 1914 had seen little distinction in types other than into fighter and reconnaissance/bomber categories, in 1917 and 1918 the non-fighter types rapidly multiplied.

The British produced a pure bomber type, the Airco DH-4, which made its appearance in 1917. Essentially a

Staaken R.VI

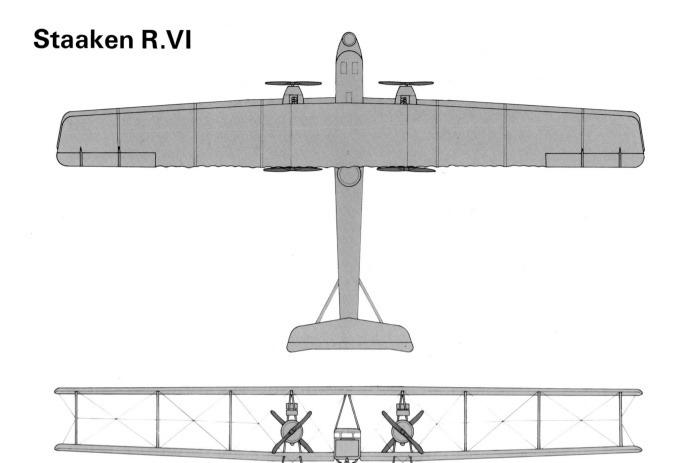

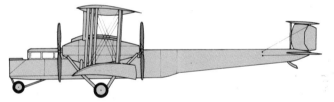

The enormous size of the R.VI is easily gauged when one remembers that each of the four propellors was some 14 feet in diameter. The aircraft illustrated is R.27/16 (Schul), which was accepted by the German air force in October 1917, and taken onto the strength of Rfa 501 on 23 January 1918. (Rfa stands for Riesenflugzeugabteilung or Giant Aeroplane Squadron.) It crashed-landed in Belgium on 7/8 March 1918.

SPECIFICATIONS

Type		seven-seater giant bomber
Engines		four Mercedes D.IVa 6-cylinder
		water-cooled inlines, 260-hp each
Armament		three or four .303-inch Lewis guns,
		plus up to 4,400 lbs of bombs
Speed	81	mph at sea level
Climb	55	minutes to 9,840 feet
Ceiling	12,470	feet
Endurance	8–12	hours
Weight	16,934	lbs (empty)
	25,269	lbs (loaded)
Span	138	feet 5½ inches
Length	72	feet 6 inches
Height	20	feet 8 inches

Amongst the most remarkable and ambitious aircraft designed in Germany during World War I were the various 'R' machines and projects, the R standing for *Riesenflugzeug* or Giant Aeroplane. Nor was the appellation Giant untrue – the R.VI was the largest aircraft operated by the Germans against Great Britain in both world wars, and its structure marked an important step forward in the design of such large aircraft.

The Zeppelin works at Staaken entered the field of giant aircraft construction in 1914, and their first design, the V.G.O. I, first flew in April 1915. The culmination of four years of wartime work was reached in the R.VI, of which 18 were built. Basically, the fuselage and wings of the R.VI were fairly orthodox by the standards of the time, the construction being mostly of wood, with fabric covering. The tailplane, however, had an unusually large amount of aluminium embodied in its structure. The tricycle undercarriage, although simple in design, had no less than 18 wheels. Although the maximum bomb-load was 4,400 lbs, this could be carried over very short ranges only, and the normal load for a long-range raid, such as night missions over London, was in the order of 2,200 lbs. The R.VI was capable of dropping Germany's largest bomb of the war, a 2,205-pounder.

The first of the new machines to be delivered was the R.25/16, in June 1917, the second machine, R.26/16, following in July. Zeppelin-Staaken built only six R.VIs, the remaining twelve being built under licence (three by Schutte-Lanz or Schul, six by Aviatik, and three by Albatros).

The first R plane raid on Great Britain was made on the night of 28/29 September 1917, and in all 28 missions against British targets were flown, the last being on 19/20 May 1918. In the course of all the combat missions flown, 11 R.VIs were lost, although only three of these were attributable to direct enemy action, the rest being caused by operational accidents. No less than three R.VIs crashed on landing in fog on the night of 9/10 May 1918.

Most successful of the R.VIs was probably the Staaken-built R.39/16, dropping 57,000 lbs of bombs in 20 missions. R.39 also dropped the only three 2,205-pounders to be dropped on Great Britain during the war, but was shot down by the Poles on 4 August 1919 near Ratibor. The aircraft was being used to fly currency from Germany to the hard-pressed and short-lived independent republic of the Ukraine at the time.

light bomber, it was followed in 1918 by a development of it, the DH-9. The former was one of the best aircraft of the war, serving in large numbers with the British and Americans. With the 375-hp Rolls Royce Eagle inline, the DH-4 had a top speed of 143 mph, a ceiling of 22,000 feet and a range of 435 miles. Its defensive armament included up to four machine guns, and its offensive load comprised 460 pounds of bombs. The performance figures would have been extremely creditable in a fighter. The DH-9 was intended as an improvement on the DH-4, but its engine power was considerably less and performance suffered accordingly. It did, however, possess the one major advantage, compared with the DH-4, of having the two crew members placed back-to-back, rather than separated in different parts of the fuselage.

The role of these light bombers was not spectacular, but they were of considerable importance in keeping up a continual harassment of the German rear areas. Their raids helped to slow down the rate at which German matériel reached the front, and they also forced the German fighter squadrons to take to the air and thus meet Allied fighting machines roving on the east of the lines. Moreover, aircraft such as the DH-4 were capable of giving a good account of themselves in an air battle. Such types were to be greatly valued—they harassed, bombed, fought, and also acted as reconnaissance machines. The larger bombers, as

BOTTOM LEFT *An aerial combat scene featuring a DH-9 light bomber and an Albatros D-V.*
BOTTOM RIGHT *A Handley Page 0/100 heavy bomber; maximum bomb load was 2,000 pounds—five times that of the DH-4.*

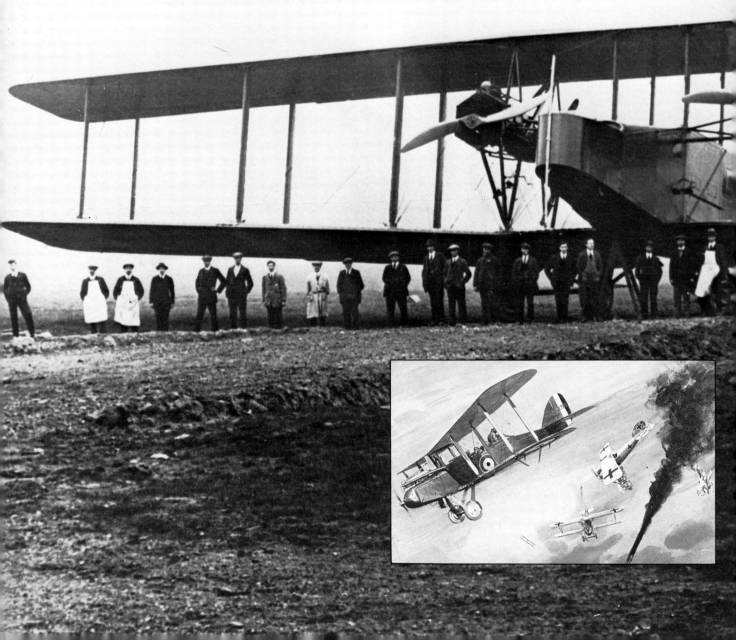

described in the next paragraph, were not so successful, however. Air theorists had vastly overestimated the effect, both on morale and on buildings, that small raids by heavy bombers would make. It was not until the advent of the great bomber fleets in 1944, and the A-bomb in 1945, that the idea of strategic bombing achieved real, practical success.

The first British version of what was intended to a strategic bomber was the Handley-Page 0/100, which entered service in September 1916. Powered by two Rolls-Royce Eagle inlines of 250-hp each, the 0/100 had a speed of 85 mph and a range of 700 miles. Defensive armament comprised three to five Lewis guns, and an offensive load

was carried of up to 2,000 pounds of bombs or a single 1,650-pounder. In 1918 Handley-Page introduced an improved version of the 0/100, the 0/400. This was powered by two Rolls-Royce Eagles of 360-hp each, and had a speed of 97½ mph and a range of 750 miles. Defensive armament included up to five Lewis guns, and the offensive load was again up to 2,000 pounds of bombs. The largest British bomber of the war was the Handley-Page V/1500. Only six had been built by the time of the Armistice. Power was provided by four Rolls-Royce Eagles developing 375 hp each. This gave the bomber a speed of 97 mph and a range of 1,200 miles. Armament was up to five Lewis guns and 7,500 pounds of bombs.

BELOW *Thirty-four men, well spaced, emphasize the Handley Page V/1500's massive 126-foot span; only six of these four-engined bombers, capable of bombing Berlin from bases in Britain, were completed before the Armistice.*

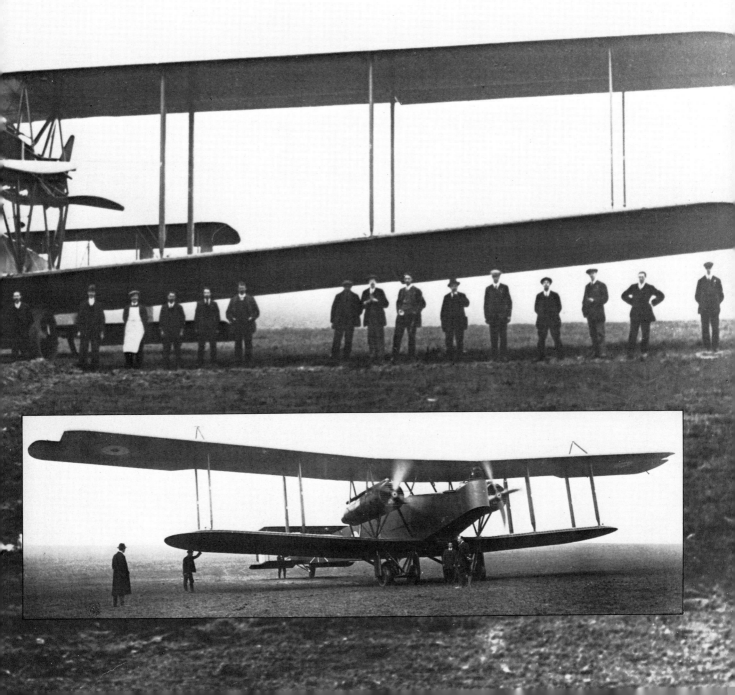

Another British type classification was that of the trench fighter, designed for ground-attack use. This was an armoured machine built to operate at low level against the German trench lines. Such fighters flew along the line of the German trenches, immune from ground fire (it was hoped) because of their armour plating, strafing the infantry in their dug-in positions. The intention behind them was twofold, firstly to kill a significant number of the opposing infantry, and secondly to reduce the efficiency of the rest by keeping them constantly on the alert. The type was developed too late to make any great impression, however. The first trench fighter was a modified Camel, but a definitive

in two versions, the 14A-2 and the 14B-2. The former was a two-seater reconnaissance machine, and the latter a bomber. Powered by a 300-hp Renault inline, the Breguet 14B-2 was a large tractor biplane capable of 121 mph, a ceiling of 19,000 feet and a range of 330 miles. Armament comprised one fixed Vickers and two or three flexible Lewis guns, plus up to 520 pounds of bombs.

Finally, on the Allied side, mention should be made of several outstanding Italian aircraft. The best of these was the Ansaldo SVA-5 strategic reconnaissance machine. This purposeful-looking tractor biplane first appeared in the autumn of 1917. Powered by an SPA-6A inline, it had an

version was the Sopwith TF-2 Salamander. This had a large amount of ammunition for the twin Vickers, and 650 pounds of armour plating. Top speed, with a Bentley BR-2 rotary, was 125 mph.

In the French camp, one of the best aircraft of the war was produced in 1918. This was the Salmson 2A-2, a reconnaissance type. Powered by a Salmson-Canton Unné water-cooled radial of 260 hp, the 2A-2 had a top speed of 115 mph and a ceiling of 20,500 feet. It was a very strong machine, and agile for its size. Its defensive armament of one fixed Vickers and two flexible Lewis guns enabled it to give a very good account of itself in combat.

France had been attached to the idea of bombing far sooner than the British, and by 1918 she had a large number of bomber squadrons. The types most commonly used in these squadrons were the Breguet 14 and the Voisin Types 6 to 10. The Voisin types had been in service since 1916. The Type 10 was powered by a 300-hp Renault inline driving a pusher propeller, and had a top speed of 84 mph and a range of 310 miles. Bomb load was up to 600 pounds. The Breguet 14 was a far superior machine, and appeared

excellent top speed of 143 mph and an endurance of four hours. Ceiling was slightly under 20,000 feet. In the field of bombing, the firm of Caproni made a significant impression, producing a large number of types between 1915 and the end of the war. Most notable of these were the Ca-32, 33, 40, 41, 42, 43, 44, 45, 46 and 47. The Ca-42 was a triplane with twin booms holding the empennage (the early term for the tail unit). Power was provided by three Fiat, Isotta-Fraschini or American Liberty inlines of 270-hp each. Armament was up to four Revelli machine guns and 3,910 pounds of bombs. Speed was 87 mph and endurance 8 hours.

The chief American contribution to the technical side of the air war lay in the field of engines. A large range of Liberty inlines was designed which, if the war had lasted into 1919, would have powered numerous types of Allied aircraft. The USA's own aircraft industry produced no worthwhile combat types of indigenous design during the war with the exception of the Curtiss America series of flying boats. The best of the series was probably the H-12 Large America. This was powered by two 275-hp Rolls-

impressive. The G-IV carried a bomb load of 1,100 pounds and was protected by two flexible Parabellum machine guns. However, in 1917-18 Germany produced some true giants. The most successful of these was the Zeppelin-Staaken R-VI. This had a wingspan of 138 feet $5\frac{3}{8}$ inches (larger than the span of the Boeing B-17 Flying Fortress) and was powered by four 260-hp Mercedes inlines. Top speed was not good at 81 mph, but its endurance capability of 10 hours and bomb load of nearly 4,000 pounds were considerable.

In the field of ground-attack aircraft, Germany produced some most interesting designs. One of the earliest of these

OPPOSITE *The Breguet 14, a French bomber capable of carrying up to 520 pounds of bombs.*
TOP *The Junkers CL-I, a German armoured trench-fighter of all-metal construction that arrived in 1918 and would have made an even greater impact had hostilities continued into 1919.*
ABOVE *The French Salmson 2A-2, a heavy reconnaissance type that also served in large numbers with the AEF.*

Royce Eagle inlines, and had a top speed of 93 mph and an endurance of 6 hours. It was used on anti-submarine patrols, and had a defensive armament of four Lewis guns and an offensive load of 460 pounds of bombs. The H-12 appeared early in 1917.

By 1918 the Germans had produced a considerable number of aircraft types designed for bombing or ground attack. The standard German bombers from 1917 onwards were the Gotha G-IV and G-V. These were large tractor biplanes, and from the spring of 1917 onwards the former took over from the Zeppelins the task of bombing Great Britain. Power was provided by two 260-hp Mercedes inlines, and although speed was not spectacular at 87 mph, ceiling and range, at 21,320 feet and 305 miles, were more

was the Halberstadt CL-II, a two-seat tractor-engined biplane that appeared in 1917 during the summer, and was soon supplemented by the improved CL-IV. Armament was three machine guns, and the type proved very effective in the German offensives of autumn 1917 and spring 1918.

One of the early pioneers of all-metal construction for aircraft was Dr Hugo Junkers, whose armoured J-I ground-attack machine appeared in the early summer of 1917. The J-I was a large two-seat tractor biplane with thick-section cantilever wings. Though heavy on the controls, the type was popular for the strength and protection of the metal construction. Its 200-hp Benz inline engine was not really enough for its considerable weight and size, and top speed was only 96 mph. But the armament of two fixed and one flexible machine gun was good. Better than the J-I, however, was the Junkers CL-I of 1918. This was developed from the all-metal D-I fighter, and was in effect a scaled-up version that took a crew of two. It was a handy, low-winged monoplane, immensely strong and a type that would have played an important part in aerial operations if the war had continued into 1919.

How they flew

Even at the very end of World War I, the art of flying was still understood only imperfectly. This lack of thorough knowledge, combined with the exigency of the training given to most novice pilots before their hasty dispatch to the sorely-pressed front, meant that many pilots lacked basic piloting and tactical skills. To remind them of what they had learned or to teach them some new development, therefore, the authorities from time to time commissioned drawings of aircraft handling and tactical factors for issue to the squadrons. These were also sent to training establishments.

Although they were a few great pilots on both sides who knew almost instinctively what to do in any given situation, in handling and in tactics, the majority of pilots desperately needed any information or hints they could get to cope with such eventualities. Illustrated are four lessons in handling and air safety (what to do in the event of engine failure, on meeting friendly aircraft in the air, looping, and when landing in hazy conditions), two lessons in tactics (keeping behind one's prey and watching out for 'the Hun in the sun') and one lesson for ground crew (keeping the elevators up when running the engine on the ground to avoid a nose-over).

The lessons were clearly useful (they were updated and expanded in scope in World War II, both by the Air Ministry and by individual squadrons or commanders).

But what was really needed was a combination of two factors: a more systematic and energetic approach to the investigation of the problems of flight; and a more intensive and prolonged training programme for novice pilots, leading on to a course in operational aspects of flying with good instructiors, rather than instructors who were for some reason or other unsuited for the front and therefore relegated to training.

However complete a pilot's training, though, the most dangerous episode in his operational career was always his first few days in combat. Here he tried to put the theory of his training into the practice of real combat, probably against more experienced opponents. It was in this phase of metamorphosis from total novice to experienced pilot that the care and hints of his co-pilots were of great use to the new man. Other pilots could give him hints on the ground, draw off a dangerous adversary in the air and perhaps set up a 'kill' for him. But most important was the disabusing of a novice of any erroneous ideas he might have–such as the utility of aerobatics in combat. Aerobatics rely heavily on relatively slow speeds combined with a long, predictable movement. Combat flying demands just the opposite–high speeds and a lack of predictability. There could be little more easy to shoot down than an aircraft at the top of a loop, hanging there almost motionless and unable to manoeuvre.

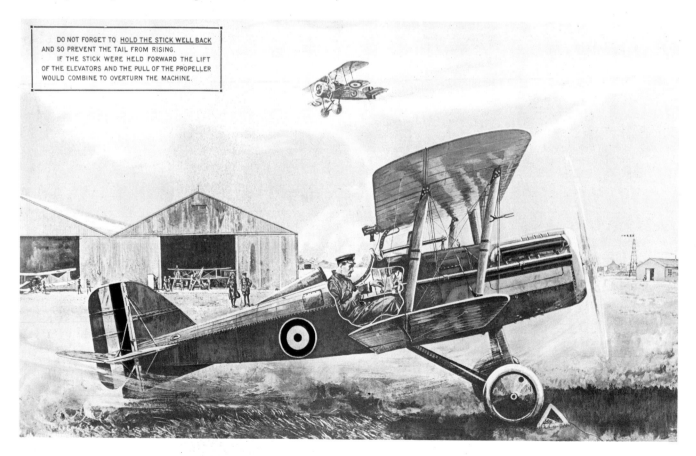

DO NOT FORGET TO HOLD THE STICK WELL BACK AND SO PREVENT THE TAIL FROM RISING.
IF THE STICK WERE HELD FORWARD THE LIFT OF THE ELEVATORS AND THE PULL OF THE PROPELLER WOULD COMBINE TO OVERTURN THE MACHINE.

OPPOSITE *The diagram demonstrates the correct position of the control stick when running the engine on the ground.*
ABOVE *'Getting Off—Engine Failure': an RE-8 has engine failure just after taking off, and wrongly tries to turn back.*
BELOW *'Rules of the Air—Meeting Another Machine': a Dolphin and two Camels meet in the air—and turn to the right.*

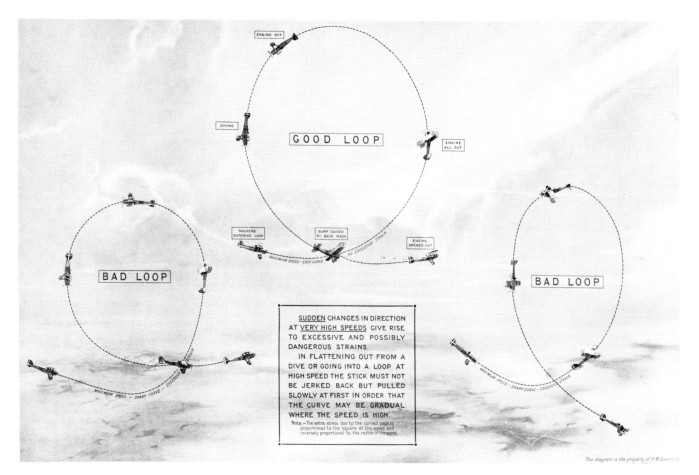

ABOVE 'Good and Bad Looping': sharp curves at high speeds can put excessive strains on an aircraft; the good loop is begun gradually, when speed is greatest.

BELOW 'Night Flying through Mist or Haze': in such conditions Holt flares are best avoided since they create intensive dazzle and blot out the ground.

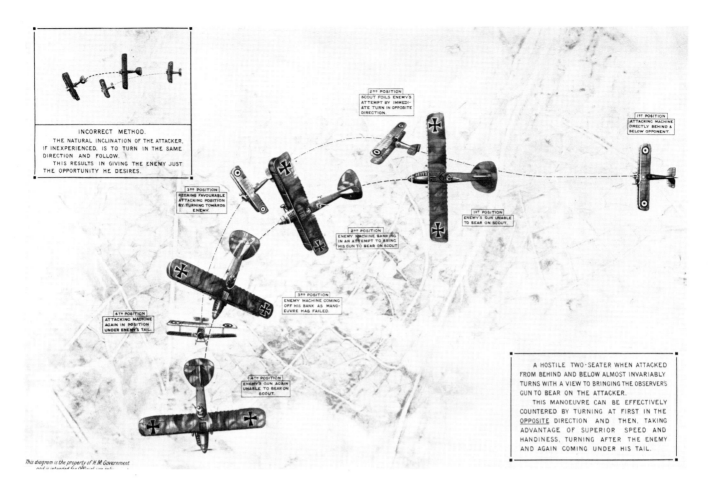

ABOVE *'Outmanoeuvred': how to deal with a hostile two-seater which, attacked from behind and below, turns in order to bring its guns to bear on the attacker.*

BELOW *'Beware the Hun in the Sun': a Fokker Dr-I triplane approaches from out of the sun while a Bristol F-2B and an Albatros D-V are engaged in combat.*

Naval Aircraft

The aircraft used in the early days of World War I for operations over the sea were of simple design and were intended merely to scout for signs of enemy activity. For this both landplanes and floatplanes were employed, and of the latter type the Sopwith Schneider and Baby were typical. Single-seat tractor biplanes, they were little more than landplanes adapted for sea use with the addition of twin floats. The British continued to use them throughout the war for scouting and anti-Zeppelin operations.

Far more importance was attached to the floatplane by the Central Powers. In Germany the main producers of floatplanes were Friedrichshafen and Hansa-Brandenburg, who also supplied most of Austria-Hungary's machines. Friedrichshafen's most successful floatplane was the FF-33, which first appeared in 1915 and was built in a bewildering number of variants for patrol and escort duties. The

OPPOSITE, LEFT *A Sopwith Pup with skid undercarriage lands on the after flight deck of HMS* Furious *in 1918. The lower picture shows the ship's fore flight deck; the hinged palisades act as a windbreak and protect the aircraft.*

OPPOSITE, RIGHT *A Short seaplane is prepared for flight.*
ABOVE *A Sopwith 1½-Strutter takes off from a platform mounted over a gun turret on board the battlecruiser HMS* New Zealand; *this technique was first used successfully in April 1918.*

FF-33l, of autumn 1916, was powered by a 150-hp Benz inline. Apart from its twin floats, it was a perfectly conventional tractor biplane and had a speed of 85 mph, an endurance of 6 hours and an armament of one fixed and one flexible machine gun.

Hansa-Brandenburg produced several very striking floatplane fighter and patrol aircraft under the design leadership of Ernst Heinkel. First came the KDW, whose biplane wings were braced with a star-shaped set of interplane struts. The type was mounted on twin floats and had a top speed of 107 mph with its 160-hp Maybach inline engine, and was armed with two fixed machine guns. The type was introduced in mid-1916 and was replaced a year later by the W-12 two-seater floatplane. Powered by a 150-hp Benz inline, the W-12 had a top speed of 100 mph and was armed with three machine guns. Heinkel's best design was the W-29, which appeared in mid-1918. This

was a twin-seat twin-float monoplane, which could achieve 109 mph on the 150 hp of its Benz inline.

Most other countries in Word War I opted for the flying-boat configuration for their seaplanes. In Austria-Hungary the most common type was the Lohner Type-L patrol and reconnaissance machine, which entered service in 1915. It was a pusher type, with the engine mounted between the wings, the lower of which rested on the hull. Speed via the 160-hp Austro-Daimler engine was 65 mph, but endurance was 4 hours and up to 440 pounds of bombs could be carried – as well as a single machine gun.

Italy adopted the same sort of configuration as the Lohner on her Macchi floatplanes. One of these, the M-5, was a single-seat fighter that had the quite remarkable top speed of 117 mph on the 160 hp of its Isotta-Fraschini inline. Armament was two machine guns.

France also followed this configuration, and the FBA

ABOVE *The Porte-Felixstowe F-2A, a British-designed flying boat.*
BELOW *An Italian Macchi M-5 flying boat with painted nose.*

OPPOSITE *Another in the series of Air Technical Diagrams: this one is entitled 'Torpedo Attack on an Anchored Ship'.*

Type-H became the most widely built flying boat in the war. The Italian-built Type-H was powered by a 180-hp Isotta-Fraschini, which gave it a top speed of 87 mph. Armament was one machine gun and it also carried a small bomb load.

Mention has already been made of the Curtiss flying boats, and from these were developed the best flying boats

ments with aircraft-carriers, the first of which, HMS *Furious*, made possible the historic landing mentioned earlier. Thereafter much ingenuity was devoted to producing aircraft that could land on the early carriers on skids which reduced their landing runs. By the end of the war the *Furious* had been converted from its early form with a taking-off platform in the bows and a landing-on platform

of the war, the British Porte-Felixstowe F-2A and F-3. The main failing of the Curtiss boats was the poor design of their hulls, and so the new aircraft's designer, Squadron Commander J. C. Porte of the Royal Naval Air Service, worked out a new hull shape and fitted more powerful engines. The result was a handsome-looking and very efficient and formidable anti-submarine and patrol boat. The F-2A was powered by two Rolls-Royce Eagles of 345 hp each, which gave it a speed of 95 mph and endurance of 6 hours; it was armed with seven Lewis guns and 460 pounds of bombs. The type entered service in 1917.

Most important of all in the long term, however, was the introduction of ship-borne aircraft. We have already seen that the first experiments were undertaken by the Americans, but the first landing on a moving ship was made by a British pilot in a Sopwith Pup on 2 August 1917. The British developed flying-off platforms on the turrets of capital ships and cruisers, but as there was no way of landing the reconnaissance aircraft back on the ship, the pilot had to ditch, which almost inevitably meant the loss of his machine. The British therefore began to conduct experi-

in the stern to a single full-length flying-deck, from which ordinary wheeled aircraft could operate.

From now on, carrier-borne aircraft using bombs and torpedoes would become the arbiters of the war at sea. The first aeroplane to be designed specifically for carrier operations was the Fairey Campania floatplane, and with the introduction of torpedo planes such as the Sopwith Cuckoo, the era of the battleship was about to end.

In reviewing the aircraft of World I, two outstanding conclusions can be drawn. Firstly, enormous strides had been made in developing the aeroplane as a reliable, multi-purpose weapon. Engineers and aerodynamicists had produced sturdy machines that could stand up to combat conditions, and theorists had decided the roles that specific types of aircraft were to play. But one's second conclusion must be that the military use of aeroplanes was still in its infancy, and that the theorists had overreached themselves during the war, and would continue to do so after 1918. It was in fact to be many years before aircraft would be able to act as a decisive arm, rather than as a lesser adjunct to forces on the ground.

Chapter Three
The Inter-War Years

World War I had been a shattering experience, and after it the world moved into a new era. Millions had died, and the cost had been all but incalculable; yet perhaps more important still, the Victorian way of life had been demolished, giving way to a new social order and a new manner of thinking.

World War I had been the 'war to end all wars', and so it was inevitable that post-war politicians would not countenance further expenditure on armaments: the world's armed forces would have to make do for the time being with the left-overs of the Great War. This post-war retrenchment was nowhere more apparent than in the air forces of the victorious Allies. A few of the experimental designs produced right at the end of the war were kept in development as test vehicles, but all other development was dropped by the military; electorates, via their governments, would not sanction further expenditure on armaments.

Of necessity this left the immediate future of aeronautical progress to the few enthusiastic manufacturers and pilots prepared to devote themselves to this labour. The next ten years, therefore, were to belong to the experimental, record, and racing aeroplane. The scene was set soon after the war by the first transatlantic flights. The first, from west to east, was achieved by a Curtiss NC-4 flying boat commanded by Lieutenant-Commander A. C. Read of the US Navy. This was an indirect crossing via the Azores, and took 12 days (16–27 May 1919). Far more significant, however, was the first non-stop crossing, by

Captain J. Alcock and Lieutenant A. Whitten-Brown in a converted Vickers Vimy bomber. They took off from Newfoundland on 14 June 1919 and crash-landed in Ireland some 16 hours later. It was to be as a result of endeavours such as this that the torch of aeronautical advance was to be kept alight in the lean 1920s. New military aircraft did, of course, make their appearance, but the significant advances were almost exclusively in the field of civil aviation, as we would now call it.

Great strides were made in the field of aircraft structures in the first few years after the end of World War I. One of the most important of these was the gradual swing away from the braced biplane formula to the cantilever monoplane, with its considerable aerodynamic advantages of reduced drag and simpler maintenance problems. The leaders in this field had emerged in Germany in the closing stages of

OPPOSITE *The Vickers Vimy, in which Alcock and Brown made the first non-stop Atlantic crossing, takes off from Newfoundland.* ABOVE *Andrei Tupolev, sixth from left, and his ANT-1 in 1923.* BELOW *A 1922 photo of the British Bullfinch single-seat fighter.* BOTTOM *The Bristol Braemar, ready just before the Armistice.*

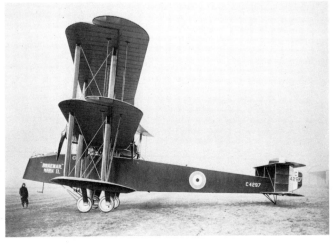

the war: Reinhold Platz of the Fokker company and Hugo Junkers. The former favoured a high-mounted thick-section cantilever wing of wooden construction and the latter a low-mounted planform, again of thick section, but made of metal and covered with corrugated metal skinning for strength and rigidity. In the long run Junkers's low wing proved superior, but not until a series of high-wing Fokkers had achieved immortality with a succession of stupendous record-breaking flights.

The main failing of the Junkers idea was not in its basic design philosophy but in the structure, with its corrugated skinning. Although an improvement on the biplane type, the skinning still resulted in a high drag factor; this was recognized by Adolph Rohrbach, who devised a structure based on strong box spars covered with a load-bearing smooth metal skin. In doing so he laid down a pattern that was to recur in most military aircraft of the late 1930s and in World War II.

As important as the introduction of the low cantilever wing was the pioneering of all-metal construction and the monocoque fuselage. Metallurgical advances in the 1920s resulted in an ever-increasing number of high-strength alloys, which allowed aeroplane structures in metal that produced both savings in structural weight and general improvements in performance. The monocoque fuselage, in which the more conventional longerons-and-frames structure with a canvas or light metal aerodynamic skinning gave way to a series of frames linked by stringers and covered with a load-bearing skinning, had appeared in the pre-World War I Deperdussin racer. It then found in-

The Vega could carry six passengers up to 900 miles at a speed of nearly 140 mph.

It is worth noting here an apparent divergence between the United States and Europe in the field of power-plants. In the United States the air-cooled radial engine was fast becoming the most important type of power-plant. It was relatively light for its power, mechanically simple, and capable of considerable development. Its main failing, however, was the large frontal area presented to the airflow, and all its attendant drag problems. In time the Americans managed to minimize these problems with the carefully tailored low-drag cowlings that became a feature of their aircraft.

In Europe there was a greater preference for the liquid-cooled inline engine, although several notable radials were developed by the French Le Rhône and British Bristol

creasing favour in the post-war years, being universally adopted in the 1930s. An important milestone in this direction was the Short Silver Streak of 1920. This was an all-metal biplane with a monocoque fuselage which started the trend in Great Britain towards metal construction.

While all-metal construction and the low monoplane planform were still in the development stage in the 1920s, the pace in the new and fast expanding field of civil transport was set by the early Fokker high-wing mono-planes such as the F-II. This design philosophy reached its culmination in the Lockheed Vega, which first appeared in 1927: of wooden construction, it had a monocoque fuselage and was powered by a 435-hp radial engine, a type that was just about to enter its heyday in the United States.

companies. The advantage of the inline, to European eyes, was its small frontal area, which allowed for a smooth, low-drag nose.

In the purely military sphere design still tended to lag behind the more advanced civilian types, and fighter aircraft were little more than World War I types updated and fitted with more powerful engines. Classic examples are the British Gloster Gamecock and the Bristol Bulldog, and the American Boeing PW-9 series and the Curtiss Hawks. The mainstays of the bombing forces, despite pressure from the strategic bombing lobby, continued to be types such as the wartime British de Havilland DH-4 and -9, and the American Martin MB-2/Curtiss NBS-1, all of which were large and ponderous biplanes.

As we have noted, it was in the field of racing and record-breaking aircraft that many of the major technical innova-

OPPOSITE, ABOVE *The Bristol Bulldog, typical of the updated World War I aircraft introduced in the 1920s.*
OPPOSITE, BELOW *The Lockheed Vega, a six-passenger aircraft that followed up the high-wing monoplane idea developed earlier by Fokker in Germany; it first appeared in 1927.*
ABOVE *The Schneider Trophy Race acted as a dynamic spur to technological progress; perhaps the most famous aircraft of that era were the Supermarine series of seaplanes developed by R. J. Mitchell: seen here is the S-6, winner in 1929 at an average speed of 329 mph. It was powered by a forerunner of the famous Rolls Royce Merlin engines that were to make a great impact in World War II.*
RIGHT *A flight of Furies; these British fighters were the first military aircraft capable of a top speed in excess of 200 mph.*
BELOW *The Comet Racer, designed by de Havilland for the England-to-Australia race of 1934, which it won at an average speed of 180 mph. In appearance it is an obvious precursor of the Mosquito bomber.*

tions were first introduced. A typical example is the development of the retractable undercarriage, which brought further advances in drag reduction. The idea did not appeal to the military at first, however, because of the complexity and weight of the retraction system. The first retractable undercarriage to appear in the United States was fitted to the Dayton-Wright RB racer of 1920; Great Britain followed in 1922 with the spectacular Bristol mid-wing monoplane racer. But is was not until the arrival of strong light-weight alloys, and incontrovertible proof had been obtained that streamlining requirements at very high speeds made retractable undercarriages necessary, that the military authorities would countenance them.

Most famous of all the air races in the years between the

two world wars was the Schneider Trophy series for sea-planes. It is hard to overestimate the importance of this series in Europe and the Pulitzer series in the United States in the way they forced technological progress along, and so kept aviation in the public eye during the austere years of the 1920s.

The two major improvements directly attributable to the Schneider Trophy races are streamlining and the development of powerful inline engines. The 1925 race was the last to be won by a biplane, the beautifully streamlined Curtiss R3C-2 flown by Jimmy Doolittle of the United States. From that date the series hotted up considerably. The Italians won the race in 1926 with a Macchi monoplane, and then the first of the justly celebrated series of monoplane seaplanes designed by a Briton, R. J. Mitchell, entered the scene. In 1927 the race was won by one of Mitchell's Supermarine entries,

ABOVE *The Junkers Ju-86, one of the dual-purpose passenger/bomber types introduced after Hitler came to power.*
BELOW *The Junkers Ju-52 all-metal trimotor, designed to serve two masters—Lufthansa and the Luftwaffe.*

the S-5, developed from the previous year's unsuccessful S-4. The S-5 was powered by an 800-hp Napier Lion, and won at a speed of 282 mph.

The aircraft were by now taking so long to build that it was decided to hold the races every other year instead of every year, so Mitchell had two years to think about his next design, the S-6. This was an impressively trim little machine (powered by the ancestor of the Rolls-Royce Merlin engine that was to win so much renown in World War II) and it won the 1929 race at a speed of 329 mph. Later this type pushed the world air-speed record up to 357·7 mph. The final Schneider Trophy race was won by Great Britain in 1931 with an improved version of the S-6, the S-6B, which went on to increase the world speed record to 407 mph.

Meanwhile the military machines of the period were considerably less rapid. In fact the premier fighter of the day, the British Hawker Fury, introduced in 1930, was the first military aeroplane in the world to have a top speed of over 200 mph. Comparable military machines of the period were the French Dewoitine D-27, with a top speed of 194 mph, and the remarkable Grumman FF-1, an American carrier-borne design. This was first flown in 1931, had a retractable undercarriage and a top speed of 201 mph.

The years 1927 and 1928 marked a prolific time for record-breaking in the sphere of long-distance flying. Quite apart from spurring on the development of powerful and reliable engines, such flights were also of special importance in proving navigation techniques and testing theories of fuel

ABOVE *The Bristol Blenheim, a light bomber developed out of the Type 142 civil aircraft.*
BELOW *The Boeing 247 transport, a true forerunner of today's low-wing, monoplane commercial aircraft, introduced in 1933.*

and so laying the foundations not only of the present world-wide air communications industry, but also of the long-range bomber techniques that were to be so much a part of the next world war. At the end of 1929 the world altitude and distance records stood at 41,794 feet (Junkers W-34) and 4,912 miles (Breguet 19).

Whereas in the 1920s the state of the aeronautical art had rested almost exclusively in the hands of the experimenters and visionaries, in the 1930s there came a universal acceptance of the developments of the previous decade, and a sudden flowering of a new generation of military aircraft. Powerful radials and inline engines of over 1,000-hp output produced speeds of 350 mph; aircraft with fixed undercarriages became oddities; metal construction and stressed skins were universally adopted, and all the design features of World War I vintage finally disappeared.

economy. First came one of the most celebrated flights of all time – Charles Lindbergh's epic solo non-stop flight from New York to Paris. He took off in his Ryan Spirit of St Louis on 20 May 1927 and landed in Paris the next day after a flight of 3,600 miles.

Then in 1928 a Junkers Bremen flew across the Atlantic under the command of Captain H. Köhl for the first non-stop east-to-west crossing – a particularly difficult feat because the prevailing winds are westerly. In May and June of the same year, a Fokker monoplane named Southern Cross was flown across the Pacific in stages from California to Australia by a crew led by Sir Charles Kingsford-Smith. These are only the most celebrated flights. At the same time, pioneers were proving long-range commercial air routes,

The pace in the early 1930s continued to be set by civil developments, both commercial and record-breaking. As we have noted, the Supermarine S-6B won the Schneider Trophy outright for Britain in 1931, and did so with a winning speed of 341 mph. Yet considerably more official effort was devoted in those days to winning a series such as the Schneider than was given to other record-breaking; we can see this by comparing the S-6B's winning speed and the world landplane speed record set up in 1932 by the American Gee Bee 7-11 Super Sportster – a mere 294 mph.

Another classic aeroplane appeared in 1934 in the form of the de Havilland Comet racer, designed for the England–Australia race of that year. The design connection between it and the Mosquito bomber of World War II is unmistakable.

During the early 1930s the leaders in the field of civil transport continued to be the Europeans, with such designs as the Fokker F-XVIII and the Junkers Ju-52/3 trimotors of 1932 and 1931 respectively. Also notable in the early days of this decade was the four-engined Junkers G-38, which paved the way for a forthcoming generation of long-range four-engined airliners, and later bombers. In fact, as Hitler's power in Germany increased, more and more of that country's newer civilian designs bore the clear signs of a dual-purpose philosophy: while there was peace they could serve as airliners, but in war they could be pressed into service as transports and bombers. Typical of this concept were the Heinkel He-111 and the Junkers Ju-86, which appeared in 1934 in civilian guise. The former was, in particular, to become one of the German Air Force's staple bombers.

But by the middle of the decade the United States had caught up with the Europeans in the development of civil aircraft and had passed them in the military field. Early in 1933 the Boeing company flew the prototype of its 247 airliner, and in the middle of the year Douglas wheeled out the prototype of their rival airliner, the DC-1. These two aeroplanes were the true ancestors of the civil aircraft we know today, with their monoplane, low-wing, monocoque construction, twin engines, retractable undercarriages, flaps on the trailing edges and variable-pitch propellers. It is interesting that the 247's precursor, the Monomail of 1930, also led to the development of two other highly significant types: these were the Boeing B-9 bomber, another all-metal, low-

On these pages are two famous training aircraft of inter-war and World War II vintage:
BELOW *The Tiger Moth, used in great numbers by the Elementary Flying Training Schools throughout World War II.*

ABOVE *The Avro Tutor, a larger and more powerful successor to the Avro 504 series of World War I and after, and predecessor of the Tiger Moth. The Tutor was fitted with several relatively sophisticated features such as brakes and adjustable seats.*

wing monoplane with a retractable undercarriage – and more than a match in performance for most 1931 fighters – and the remarkable Boeing P-26 fighter. The latter was a small single-engined monoplane fighter with a fixed, spatted undercarriage and capable of 235 mph, which was some 30 mph faster than contemporary European fighters in 1931.

Although it was a good design, the Boeing 247 never enjoyed the popularity of its Douglas rival, which was quickly developed via the DC-2 into the 'immortal' DC-3 of 1935. This was basically the same design as the DC-1, and could carry 21 passengers at 170 mph for 500 miles. The emergence of these American designs spurred Europe's designers into fresh activity, but their answers could not match the Americans on commercial grounds. We have already mentioned the Heinkel He-111 and the Junkers Ju-86, and we should also mention their British counterpart, the Bristol 142. Smaller than either of the American airliners, it was later developed into one of the first truly modern light bombers, the Bristol Blenheim.

Although Germany was forbidden by the terms of the Treaty of Versailles, signed in June 1919, to possess military aircraft, the advent of the Nazi regime in 1933 altered that. Hitler was not then ready to declare his intentions openly, but he ordered the clandestine formation of a new air force, the Luftwaffe, from the scattered elements that had kept German air-mindedness alive in the 1920s. He also commanded the nation's aircraft manufacturers to start developing military types for the day when German rearmament would be revealed. This was not an unduly difficult problem as German designers had been operating in other countries,

and soon the Luftwaffe was the best-equipped air force in the world.

The type selected as the Luftwaffe's standard fighter was the Messerschmitt Bf-109, a clean-lined, low-wing, single-engined monoplane with a retractable undercarriage. Design was started in 1933 and the first prototype flew in the autumn of 1935. The Bf-109B, armed with three 7·9-mm machine guns or two machine guns and one 20-mm cannon, entered service in 1937 and by the following year had proved itself a very formidable fighter in the Spanish Civil War (1936–39).

The Luftwaffe had also developed, in conjunction with the Army, a tactical doctrine of using bombers as 'flying artillery' for the Army, and in this field the Luftwaffe's equivalent of a light bomber, the Junkers Ju-87 Stuka, was to win great notoriety. Junkers's Swedish office had designed a dive-bomber as early as 1928 (the K-47), but it was the

notably Russia, Sweden, Switzerland and Holland, and now it was mostly a question of getting German aircraft factories ready for full-time military production.

Germany's chief advantage in building up her new air force was that she did not have an expensive legacy of old types needing to be used up. As soon as the existence of the new force was revealed in 1935, German manufacturers could start turning out up-to-date machines for immediate adoption. A few older types were produced at first to tide the Luftwaffe over until the new designs could enter widespread service. Such types were the Arado Ar-68 biplane fighter, the Dornier Do-13 bomber, the Heinkel He-51 biplane fighter and the Junkers Ju-52/3 bomber. But more modern designs were already under construction in 1935,

arrival of Ernst Udet, a celebrated World War I ace and flying celebrity, with an American Curtiss adapted for dive-bombing, that decided the Germans that dive-bombing was the optimum method of delivering bombs with great accuracy and with devastating psychological effect. Design of the Stuka began in 1934. It emerged in 1935, a compact and purposeful machine, single-engined, with a low inverted-gull wing and spatted undercarriage. Its bomb-load consisted of either a 550- or 1,100-pound bomb. The type entered service early in 1937.

Germany had few ideas about strategic bombing after the death of its chief proponent, General Wever, in an accident in 1936, and so her bomber fleet consisted almost exclusively of medium bombers. It was to be a decision that Germany

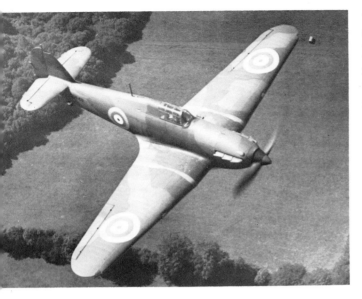

was to regret when she invaded Russia in 1941. The Germans used three main types of bomber in the war: the Heinkel He-111 already mentioned, which entered service in late 1936 (2,200-pound bomb-load); the Dornier Do-17, which entered service in 1937 (2,200-pound bomb-load), and the Junkers Ju-88, which entered service in 1939 (4,000-pound bomb-load) and was one of the most versatile and useful aircraft of the war.

At last recognizing that the threat of war was looming ever closer, the rest of Europe rather belatedly joined the arms race. Great Britain's air force was in the mid-1930s desperately out of date: her fighter mainstay was the 230-mph Gloster Gauntlet biplane, which had an open cockpit and a fixed undercarriage – though the slightly more modern 250-mph Gloster Gladiator, which had an enclosed cockpit, was about to enter service (early in 1937). Aware of the

OPPOSITE *German Junkers Ju-87 Stukas, or dive-bombers, in the colours of the Condor Legion during the Spanish Civil War.*
ABOVE LEFT *The British Hawker Hurricane, a low-wing monoplane fighter; like the Stukas, it had an enclosed cockpit.*
LEFT *One of the spearheads of Britain's out-of-date air force in the mid/late 1930s was this aircraft, the Gloster Gladiator, a biplane fighter.*
BELOW LEFT *An Italian development, the Cant Z-506 seaplane, used in the war for reconnaissance and as a torpedo-bomber.*

inadequacies of these two fighters, the Royal Air Force set about acquiring more modern types. The first to enter service, in 1937, was the eight-machine-gun, 325-mph Hawker Hurricane, an angular but sturdy low-wing monoplane with an enclosed cockpit and a retractable undercarriage. It was joined in service in 1938 by the superlative eight-gun, 350-mph Supermarine Spitfire, a descendant of R. J. Mitchell's Schneider Trophy racers.

Britain's bombers were little better than her fighters in the mid-1930s. Her standard light bomber was the Hawker Hart biplane, a two-seater version of the Fury fighter capable of carrying 500 pounds of bombs a distance of 470 miles. The standard heavy bomber was the Handley-Page Heyford biplane, capable of carrying 2,800 pounds of bombs

Vickers Supermarine Spitfire I

SPECIFICATION

Type		single-seat interceptor fighter
Engine		Rolls-Royce Merlin III 12-cylinder Vee liquid-cooled inline, 1,030-hp at take-off
Armament		eight ·303-inch Browning machine guns with 300 rounds per gun
Speed	362	mph at 19,000 feet
Initial climb rate	2,500	feet per minute
Climb	9	minutes 24 seconds to 20,000 feet
Ceiling	31,900	feet
Range	395	miles
Weight	4,810	pounds (empty)
	6,200	pounds (loaded)
Span	32	feet 10 inches
Length	29	feet 11 inches
Height	12	feet 3 inches

The Supermarine Spitfire I illustrated was a machine of No. 19 Squadron, RAF Fighter Command, operating from Duxford in Cambridgeshire. QV were the unit code letters of 19 Squadron from the beginning to the end of World War II. The first service Spitfires were allocated to this squadron in 1938, when its code was WZ.

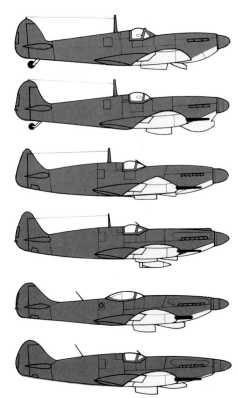

SPITFIRE IIA *improved engine giving improved climb and ceiling; 170 Mk IIs completed as IIBs with two 20-mm cannon and four ·303-inch machine guns.*

SPITFIRE VC *introduced in March 1941 with more powerful engine giving better performance; could carry bombs and was used as a fighter-bomber.*

SPITFIRE VII *extended wings for high altitude work and two-stage Merlin to give a speed of over 400 mph at 25,000 feet; ceiling 43,000 feet.*

SPITFIRE XII *first Griffon-engined model; fighter-bomber that could climb to 20,000 feet in 6 minutes 42 seconds; ceiling 40,000 feet; introduced spring 1943.*

SPITFIRE XIVE *cut-down fuselage and all-round vision bubble canopy; speed 448 mph, range 850 miles and ceiling 44,500 feet; introduced January 1944.*

SPITFIRE 21 *introduced February 1944; features stronger wing; speed 454 mph, armament four 20-mm cannon and up to 1,000 pounds of bombs.*

The Supermarine Spitfire, perhaps the most famous aircraft ever built, was produced in greater numbers than any other British aircraft, and was the only aircraft to remain in production throughout World War II in Great Britain.

Developed by R. J. Mitchell from his series of floatplane racers, the first Spitfire, K/5054, flew on 5 March 1936, and was an immediate success. Deliveries to the RAF began in 1938, and by the time production ended, 20,334 Spitfires and 2,408 Seafires, the naval version, had been built in 26 major marks. In that time speeds had been improved by nearly 100 mph, ceiling to 44,000 feet, range to nearly 1,000 miles, and armament to two or four 20-mm cannon, two or four machine guns and 1,000 pounds of bombs.

The most numerous model was the Mk V, of which 6,479 were built, followed by the Mk IX (5,665), Mk VIII (1,658), Mk I (1,566) and Mk XVI (1,054); 1,220 examples of the Seafire Mk III were built. Originally designed for the superlative Merlin engine, the Spitfire from the Mk XII (excepting the PR XIII and Mk XVI) onwards was powered by the Rolls-Royce Griffon, a higher-powered development of the Merlin.

Chief of the Spitfire's many virtues was its superb handling characteristics: its excellent manoeuvrability, good climb, fair turn of speed and adequate visibility, all combined to make it a good fighter and later fighter-bomber. Its main disadvantage was its heavy aileron control, especially at high speed.

some 920 miles. But in 1937 the Bristol Blenheim entered service. This was capable of carrying 1,000 pounds of bombs at 240 mph up to 1,000 miles, and was for its time a good machine. It was soon joined in service by the new generation of medium and heavy bombers: the Vickers Wellington (4,500 pounds of bombs, 220 mph, 1,100 miles); the Armstrong-Whitworth Whitley (7,000 pounds of bombs, 190 mph, 1,250 miles), and the Handley-Page Hampden (4,000 pounds of bombs, 250 mph, 1,200 miles).

The French started too late for any of their new designs to alter the course of the war in 1940. Their best fighter was the Dewoitine 520, a handy little monoplane armed with four machine guns and a cannon, and capable of 340 mph. And although exciting new designs such as the Amiot 350 series bomber and the Lioré et Olivier LeO-45 bomber had been produced in small numbers, the backbone of the

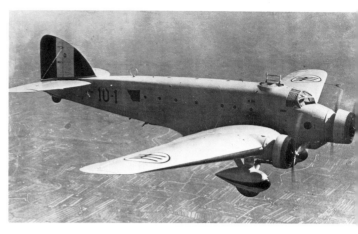

ABOVE *The Italian Savoia-Marchetti SM-81 Pipistrello (Bat) bomber, which flew for the first time in 1935 and was predominant in Mussolini's Ethiopian campaign.*

French bomber force was still composed of such obsolete types as the Amiot 143, the Bloch 200 and the Farman 222 – unwieldy, slab-sided monsters of little practical use.

Italy was little better off, having drawn the wrong conclusions from her experiences in both the Spanish Civil War and the invasion of Ethiopia. In Spain her nimble Fiat CR-32 and -42 biplanes had been able to give a good account of themselves against the poorly handled Russian Polikarpov I-15 biplane and I-16 monoplane fighters, and in Ethiopia her Savoia-Marchetti SM-79 and -81 bombers had ruled the skies. Yet despite their successes the Italians took more than one false direction: even in the first of their monoplane fighters, for example, they went for agility rather than speed, protection and firepower.

ABOVE *Andrei Tupolev's ANT-6, a heavy long-range bomber seen here in 1930 mounted on skis; obsolete by the outbreak of war, they served mostly as paratroop transports.*
BELOW *The Polikarpov I-16, standard Russian fighter in the 1930s, armed with two 20-mm cannon and two machine guns.*

Russia had developed the giant Tupolev ANT-6 heavy bomber in the 1930s, then in 1939 her bomber forces were equipped with the excellent Tupolev SB-2 light bomber, which had performed well in Spain, and the equally good Ilyushin DB-3. Russia's standard fighter was still the I-16 monoplane, which had been very advanced on its introduction in 1935 – indeed it was the first low-wing monoplane single-seat fighter in the world to be fitted with a retractable undercarriage. By 1939, however, it was obsolescent.

Such, then, were the aircraft flown by the major combatant powers when war began in Europe in the autumn of 1939. To summarize the situation: Germany had a modern and powerful tactical air force; Britain had two good fighter types and adequate bombers, but was only just beginning to get into her stride; France had left it too late; Italy had some good aircraft but had not devoted sufficient thought to the needs of the future, and Russia had good bombers but poor fighters, and needed the jolt of her initial defeats – over Finland in 1940 and over her own territory in 1941 – to put her on the right path. Other nations, such as Holland, had some interesting types, but possessed too few of them.

It should be mentioned, too, before we close this chapter, that on 27 August 1939, only five days before Germany invaded Poland, the flight took place of the world's first true jet aeroplane, the Heinkel He-178, powered by a turbojet (Heinkel S-3b) designed by Pabst von Ohain. A new era in aircraft propulsion was not far away.

On the eve of the war, the world air records stood at 469·14 mph (Bf-109R) for speed, 56,046 feet (Caproni 161) for altitude, and 7,148 miles (Vickers Wellesley) for distance.

ABOVE *A spectacular view of the Russian ANT-6 bomber on exercise carrying biplane and monoplane fighters.*
LEFT *The Italian Fiat CR-32 single-seat biplane fighter, adequate in the Spanish Civil War but obsolete soon after.*

Air Warfare 1939-45

A Chronology

THE SYMBOL ☐ DENOTES ACTIVITY OVER A PERIOD OF TIME

1939

SEPTEMBER

1   Germany invades Poland. Luftwaffe provides massive aerial support.

3   Britain and France declare war on Germany.

OCTOBER

28   First German aircraft brought down on British soil.

NOVEMBER

10   US General H. H. Arnolds calls for superbomber (later B-29).

18   Germans start sowing magnetic mines in British waters.

30   Russia invades Finland. Air-raids on Finnish towns.

1940

MARCH

16   First British civilian bombing casualties.

APRIL

9   German invasion of Denmark and Norway, supported by massive paratroop and airlift operations.

15   British bombers attack Stavanger in first inland attack of war.

MAY

10   German forces invade Belgium, Holland, Luxembourg and France. Daring airborne attack on Fort Eben-Emael.

14   Germans bomb old quarter of Rotterdam, almost totally destroying it.

15   First major RAF bombing raid on German industry, in Ruhr area.

JUNE

10   Italy declares war on the Allies.

11   Malta attacked for first time; RAF bombs targets in Turin.

JULY

☐   Intensification of German raids on airfields and ports in southern Britain.

AUGUST

2   'Adlertag', opening of Battle of Britain, fixed by Goering for 10 August, later postponed to 13th.

15   Heaviest day's fighting in Battle of Britain.

24   First bombs fall on central London.

SEPTEMBER

7   Main effort of Luftwaffe switched from airfields to central London; beginning of Blitz.

OCTOBER

6   First major night raid on London.

NOVEMBER

11   Fleet Air Arm raid on Taranto.

14   Major bombing attack on Coventry.

25   Prototype Mosquito bomber makes first flight.

1941

FEBRUARY

10   First raid by British 4-engined bombers (Short Stirlings).

24   First raid by Avro Manchester 2-engined bombers.

MARCH

10   Handley-Page Halifax 4-engined bombers make their first raid.

APRIL

15   Igor Sikorsky makes first true, controlled helicopter flight, in USA.

MAY

10   Last major air-raid on London for three years.

15   Prototype British jet aircraft, Gloster-Whittle E/29, flies for first time.

20   Beginning of German airborne invasion of Crete.

26   RAF Catalina flying boat locates the *Bismarck*. She is then crippled and sunk.

JUNE

20   US Army Corps becomes US Army Air Forces.

22   Germany invades USSR. Luftwaffe strikes ahead of advancing land forces.

NOVEMBER

☐   RAF gains complete air superiority over Western Desert.

DECEMBER

7   Surprise Japanese attack on US Pacific Fleet in Pearl Harbor.

10   British capital ships *Prince of Wales* and *Repulse* sunk by Japanese aircraft.

28   Heavy Japanese air-raids on targets in Philippines.

1942

FEBRUARY

2   German battlecruisers *Scharnhorst* and *Gneisenau* escape to Germany via English Channel despite desperate Fleet Air Arm Swordfish efforts to halt them.

APRIL

5   Japanese aircraft sink HM cruisers *Dorsetshire* and *Cornwall* off Ceylon.

9   Japanese aircraft sink HM carrier *Hermes*.

18   Doolittle raid on Tokyo.

MAY

30   First RAF 1,000-bomber raid made on Cologne.

JUNE

12   USAAF Liberators bomb Ploesti oilfields in Rumania.

24   1,000-bomber raid on Bremen.

JULY

1   First USAAF 8th Air Force B-17s land in Britain.

4   First USAAF air-raid on occupied Europe.

AUGUST

15   RAF Pathfinder Force formed to help bomber crews.

17   8th Air Force B-17s make their first raid.

SEPTEMBER

21   Prototype B-29 Superfortress makes maiden flight.

25   Daring raid by Mosquitoes on Gestapo headquarters in Oslo.

OCTOBER

1   First American jet aircraft, Bell XP-59A, makes maiden flight.

10   Beginning of last major air offensive on Malta.

1943

JANUARY

27   US aircraft raid Germany for first time.

30   First daylight raid on Berlin, by Mosquitoes.

MARCH

5   Prototype Gloster Meteor fighter makes maiden flight.

MAY

16   'Dambuster raid' by RAF Lancasters of 617 Squadron.

23   RAF Bomber Command drops its 100,000th ton of bombs on Germany.

20 Beginning of RAF shuttle raids starting in Britain and ending in North Africa.

28 Air reconnaissance reveals evidence of missile work at Peenemunde.

JULY

9 Invasion of Sicily launched with large-scale airborne landings.

29 Massive raid on Hamburg virtually destroys city.

AUGUST

1 Heavy raid on Ploesti by the USAAF.

17 RAF bombs and severely damages Peenemunde experimental station.

SEPTEMBER

10 Italian battleship *Roma* sunk by German air-launched guided bomb.

OCTOBER

14 Disastrous USAAF raid on Schweinfurt.

DECEMBER

13 USAAF sends out 1,462 aircraft in largest raid of war to date.

1944

JANUARY

9 Prototype Lockheed XP-80 jet fighter makes maiden flight.

FEBRUARY

15 Monte Cassino Abbey totally destroyed by bombing.

25 Large-scale US raid on Regensburg.

MARCH

4 US bombers, escorted by fighters, raid Berlin.

APRIL

15 Priorities for Allied bombers switched to German transport system.

24 First B-29 bomber for strategic bombing of Japan arrives in China.

JUNE

6 D-Day invasion of France launched. Massive aerial support.

15 Beginning of US strategic raids on Japan from China.

JULY

17 Napalm used operationally for first time.

25 Massive carpet-bombing raid to open way for American ground forces breaking out at Avranches.

OCTOBER

12 First B-29 for shorter-range raids on Japan lands on Saipan.

NOVEMBER

12 RAF Lancasters sink German battleship *Tirpitz* at her moorings.

The RAF Hurricane used in World War II by Group Captain Douglas Bader.

1945

JANUARY

1 Last major raid of war made by the Luftwaffe.

FEBRUARY

13 Beginning of destruction of Dresden in three days' bombing.

25 Largest raid on Tokyo to date causes enormous damage.

APRIL

6 Massive Japanese 'kamikaze' raid on US invasion fleet off Okinawa.

MAY

8 Unconditional German surrender.

AUGUST

6 First atom bomb dropped on Hiroshima.

9 Second atom bomb dropped on Nagasaki.

SEPTEMBER

2 Japanese instrument of surrender signed aboard US battleship *Missouri* in Tokyo Bay.

Chapter Four
World War II

The pattern of air operations on the German side became apparent as early as the invasion of Poland. The PZL P-11 fighters of the Polish Air Force, which with their shoulder-mounted gull wing and cannon armament had been in the forefront of fighter development when they were introduced in 1932, were obsolete compared with the Bf-109s of the Luftwaffe; consequently, for all the gallantry of their pilots, they were soon knocked out of the way. This allowed the German bombers to roam the skies virtually unmolested, destroying the Polish rear areas and breaking all Polish rail and telephone communications. At the front itself, close-support aircraft such as the Henschel Hs-126 and the Stukas blasted the way open for the German armoured and infantry formations. There was still much hard fighting on the ground but, after the attentions of the German bombers, any prolonged resistance by the Poles was out of the question. The few Polish aircraft left after the initial onslaught were flown to sanctuary in then-neutral Rumania.

The Western Front

Wilhelmshaven. Each was armed defensively with six ·303-inch machine guns, and it was hoped that by flying in a tight 'box' the various aircraft would be able to cover each other. The formation was intercepted off Heligoland by Messerschmitt Bf-109 and -110 fighters.[1] Ten of the Wellingtons were shot down and three others severely damaged in broadside attacks by the German fighters. It was experiences such as these that convinced the Royal Air Force that there was no future in daylight raids, and that night operations would result in lower, more acceptable casualties.

In April 1940 the Germans sprang a major surprise on the Allies by invading Denmark and Norway. As well as the

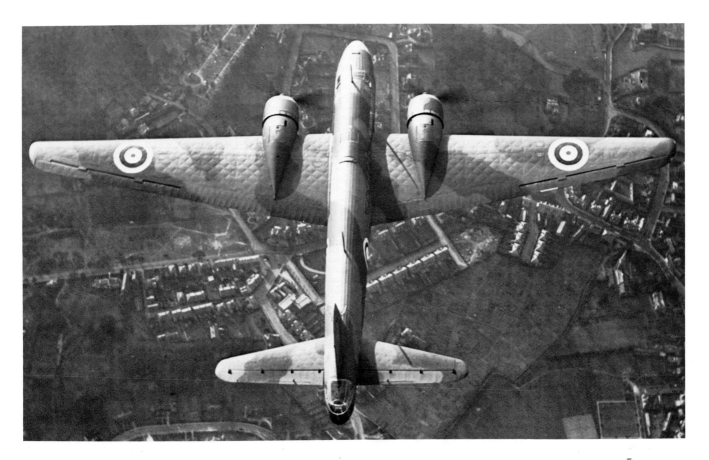

OPPOSITE *A Henschel Hs-126 close-support aircraft of the type that cleared a path for the German armour in Poland in 1939.* TOP *A Junkers Ju-88, one of the war's most versatile machines.* ABOVE *A British Wellington bomber; in 1939–40 these suffered heavy losses in daylight raids over Germany.*

In the first winter of the war, air operations on the Western Front were as sporadic as the ground operations of the 'phoney war', and there were few means of assessing the relative merits of the men and matériel on each side. It was not until the German offensive of May 1940 that the Allies were to learn how under-equipped their air forces still were.

One fact did become apparent in the first few months of the war, however: that the defensive armament of British bombers was wholly inadequate. On 18 December 1939, 24 Wellington bombers set off to raid the German fleet in

more conventional seaborne invasion, there was an unconventional airborne assault; German paratroops were dropped ahead of the main forces to secure airfields and other strategic points, and were quickly backed up by what we would now call air-portable troops, *i.e.* light infantry flown in by transport aircraft. By the daring use of such forces the Germans were able to secure their objectives at the cost of considerably fewer casualties than they would otherwise have done. As it was, the losses to the 'conventional' forces, in particular the naval units, were heavy.

Then came the German onslaught into Holland, Belgium and France. And here there was another surprise: glider-

---

[1] The Bf-110 was a twin-engined 'destroyer', designed to intercept bombers, at which it proved excellent, and not as a long-range escort fighter, the role that was later pressed on it and in which it proved a failure.

Blitzkrieg Tactics

The combined land/air *Blitzkrieg* (lightning war) tactics that made so great a contribution to the German successes early in the war were the logical conclusion of the storm troop tactics developed by General Hutier for the German Army's last offensives in 1918, as Wilhelm II's *Reich* made its last attempts at victory in World War I. Hutier's tactics envisaged a first wave of storm troops who advanced as quickly as possible, bypassing major obstacles, towards the enemy's gun line and communications. Once these had been reached and captured, the slower troops following up in the rear could take their time in reducing

the obstacles that had been left by the first wave and mopping up any other opposition. The *Blitzkrieg* was essentially similar.

The tactics were carefully thought out, and the individual components thoroughly tested, in the Spanish Civil War. Instead of infantry storm troopers, the first wave was now to be composed of armoured fighting vehicles, with armoured cars reconnoitring at the very spearhead and tanks forming the main striking power of the initial thrust. Carefully controlled artillery, which had provided the best means of removing obstacles in World War I, was now supplemented and almost totally replaced by tactical air power. Aircraft opened the way for the armoured spearhead and prevented enemy reinforcements from moving up, while the conventional forces moving up in the rear

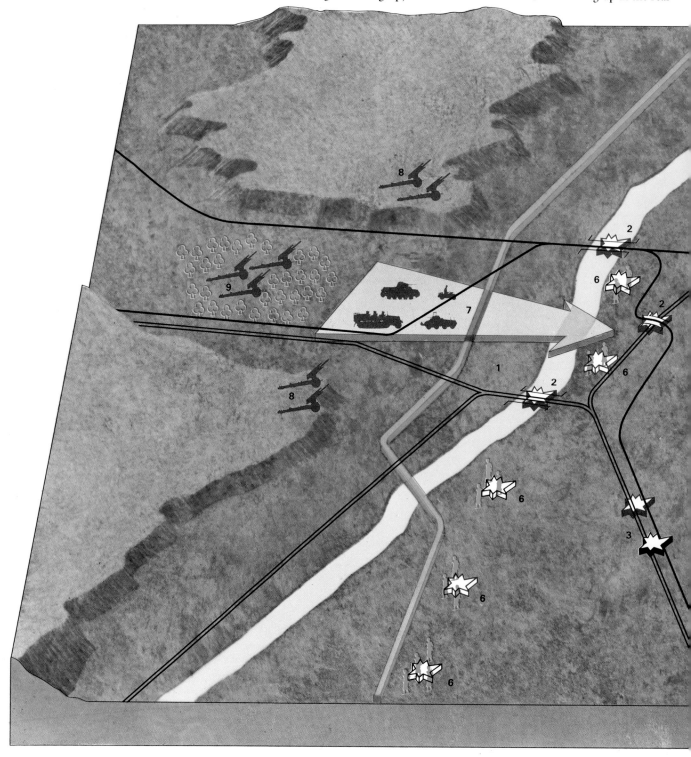

mopped up and consolidated as quickly as they could. The armour meanwhile pressed on as far as it could.

The key to the successful combination of armoured and air power was the forward controller (1), who was in constant touch with the aircraft supporting his ground forces and passed on the requirements of the ground commander, and in turn passed back the fruits of any reconnaissance in front of the ground forces. As well as pressing on as fast as they could, the Germans also wished to cut off all the enemy forces they could, and to this effect Junkers Ju-87 Stukas would be called in to dive-bomb and destroy bridges in the enemy's rear (2), to prevent them from escaping. At the same time, Heinkel He-111 and Dornier Do-17 medium bombers, perhaps aided by Stukas, would cut

the road and rail links to the front (3), both to prevent enemy reinforcements and *matériel* reaching the front and to halt any large-scale evacuation of front line forces. Any reserves would also be attacked by the bombers, and also by Messerschmitt Bf-109 and Henschel Hs-123 fighters and ground-attack aircraft (4). Major towns and any marshalling yards behind the front would also be bombed (5). When the actual assault was sent in, fighters and ground-attack aircraft would harass the front line opposition (6) to soften it up for the assault (7). German anti-aircraft guns on the high ground would prevent enemy aircraft hampering the German thrust (8), and further guns concealed in woods protected the German communications (9), the enemy's AA guns having been knocked out by Stukas (10).

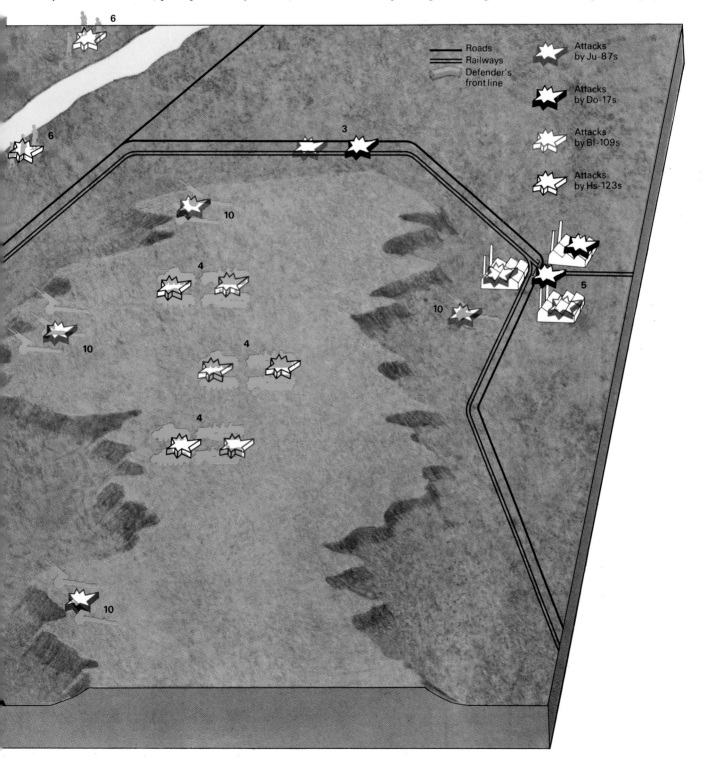

borne troops landed on the top of the key Belgian fortress of Eben-Emael and neutralized its defences. Otherwise the German invasion, following the pattern of the attack on Poland, consisted chiefly of deep thrusts by the armoured columns while the Luftwaffe's fighters held off the Allied bombers and the Stukas blew a way open for the tanks. It was a carefully thought-out and rehearsed example of how best to use tactical air power. The Allies, with no combat experience that might have helped the pilots – or at least shown up the shortcomings of their aircraft – suffered heavily. A classic example was the slaughter of all the Fairey Battle light bombers sent to destroy the Maastricht bridges on 10 May 1940. These aircraft were totally obsolete and stood no chance against the experienced German defences.

On the 20th of the same month, the situation was so desperate that 71 Battles were sent to attack German pontoon bridges over the Meuse at Sedan. Forty were shot down.

The Battle of France merely confirmed that as yet the Germans were not to be mastered in the use of tactical air power. Their bombers were fast and carried an ample bomb-load for the tasks allotted them; the Stukas could operate to devastating effect when they had air superiority, and the Messerschmitt fighters, with their heavy-cannon armament and armour protection, were equal to the British Hurricanes and the French Dewoitines and Bloch 151s and 152s that were sent against them.

But the summer of 1940 exposed failings in Germany's pre-war planning. If Britain were to be invaded, the Luft-

ABOVE *In the Western Desert campaign a flight of Fairey Albacore torpedo-bombers is seen on patrol near the Libyan coast.*
LEFT *British troops examine a Messerschmitt Bf-109F fighter shot down in the desert.*
OPPOSITE *A Dornier Do-17 bomber over London during the Blitz.*

gradually phased into a new career as a heavily-armed (four 20- or two 40-mm cannon and bombs or rockets) ground-attack and anti-tank machine. And in an effort to match the new model of the Bf-109, the F mark, the Mark V Spitfire (the next major version to see widespread service) was fitted with two 20-mm cannon and four machine guns, plus an improved engine that now gave it a speed of 375 mph at 13,000 feet. Still later models were given provision for an armament of four 20-mm cannon, or two cannon and four machine guns, or two cannon and two ·5-inch machine guns, plus up to 2,000 pounds of bombs. And with ever increased engine power, first with the Merlin, and then with a development of the Merlin, the Griffon, speed rose to 404 mph in the Mark LF IX, to 448 mph in the Mark XIV and to 454 mph in the Mark 24. At the same time combat range was increased from an initial 500 miles in the role of a pure interceptor to, late in the war, nearly 1,000 miles (with drop tanks) when the Spitfire served as a fighter-bomber.

Similar changes were made to the Bf-109. Armament on the Bf-109E was two 20-mm cannon and two 7·9-mm machine guns plus up to 550 pounds of bombs, rising by the end of the war, on the Bf-109G-6, to a variable combination of 30- and 20-mm cannon, 12·7-mm machine guns and bombs. Performance was also raised by fitting more powerful Daimler-Benz 601 engines and then the newer 605. Speed rose from 354 mph at 12,300 feet on the E-1 to 390 mph at 22,000 feet on the F-3 and to 452 mph at 19,685 feet on the K-4, one of the last variants to be produced in the war. All in all the Spitfire and Bf-109 had closely parallel careers, each being updated mark by mark in an effort to win a qualitative superiority over the other side, finally ending the war as vastly improved fighter-bomber versions of the original interceptors.

With the failure of the Luftwaffe to crush the Royal Air Force in the Battle of Britain, and the failure of the Blitz to crush civilian morale and British industry, new and vital decisions could be taken about the future conduct of the war. One such was the implementation of a plan to attack the Axis forces on the ground, and to do so not in Europe – this was recognized as impossible after the all-too-recent debacles in France, Norway and elsewhere – but in North Africa, where the opposition was seen to be weaker.

The air side of the North African campaign opened in a somewhat haphazard fashion, yet by 1943 this theatre had taken over the lead in the development of aerial tactics. In the beginning, in late 1940, the theatre was the repository of Britain's obsolete aircraft and Italy's front-line but obsolescent types. The war was initially spasmodic, then built up in intensity and in the quality of the aircraft available to both sides, particularly after February 1941 as Rommel and his Afrika Korps made their appearance. Soon an intensive air campaign was being waged – and one that was remarkable for World War II in that it was almost purely military (there being few worthwhile civilian targets).

waffe must first neutralize her aerial defences. This was a strategic not a tactical operation, and the Germans simply did not possess the aircraft for it. The Messerschmitts carried only enough fuel for 20 minutes of combat over southern England; consequently the bombers could not rely on being escorted much beyond Kent, Sussex and Hampshire, and without an escort they, in particular the Stukas, were easy meat for RAF Fighter Command's Hurricanes. Moreover, the Bf-109, even in the E or Emil model by then in service, found a worthy opponent in the Supermarine Spitfire, especially once the latter had been fitted with a constant-speed propeller to take full advantage of the power available from its Rolls-Royce Merlin engine at all operating altitudes.[2] The British had also learned the tactical lessons of their defeat in France: no longer did they fly in rigid formations, but rather in easy-to-maintain and tactically superior pairs or groups of pairs.

The Battle of Britain was a major turning point for both sides: it showed the Germans that they could not undertake a strategic role with the aircraft they then had; and it showed the British that they could take on and beat the nation that had overrun most of northern Europe. Of course, the British had also learned other lessons. In particular, it was apparent that the Hurricane was nearing the end of its usefulness as a first-line interceptor, and that the eight-gun armament of the Spitfire left much to be desired. So the Hurricane was

[2] The constant-speed propeller was developed to obtain maximum benefit from the ever-increasing power of piston engines. It automatically adjusted itself to make the best use of engine revolutions at varying altitudes. This was of special benefit to interceptor fighters as they climbed to engage the enemy.

ABOVE *A torpedo-armed Fairey Swordfish, one of the survivors of World War II, stands by with wings folded.*

BELOW *A Swordfish drops her torpedo; these obsolete yet tough aircraft did notable work in the struggle against the U-boats.*

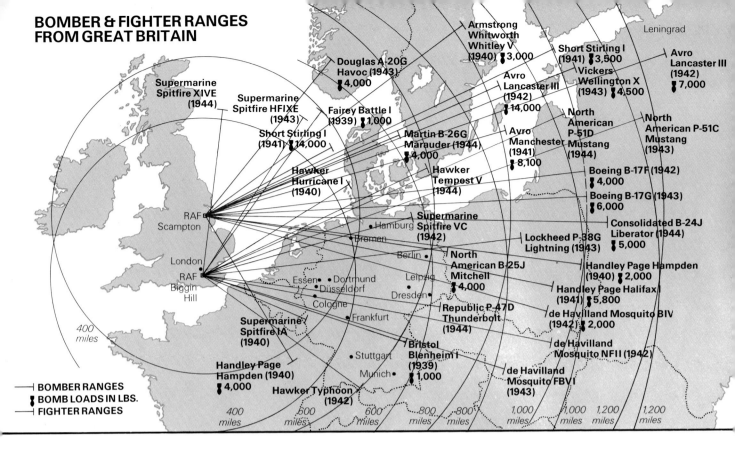

BOMBER & FIGHTER RANGES FROM GREAT BRITAIN

Leningrad

Supermarine Spitfire XIVE (1944)

Supermarine Spitfire HFIXE (1943)

Fairey Battle I (1939) ▌1,000

Douglas A-20G Havoc (1943) ▌4,000

Armstrong Whitworth Whitley V (1940) ▌3,000

Short Stirling I (1941) ▌3,500

Vickers Wellington X (1943) ▌4,500

Avro Lancaster III (1942) ▌7,000

Short Stirling I (1941) ▌14,000

Avro Lancaster III (1942) ▌14,000

Martin B-26G Marauder (1944) ▌4,000

Avro Manchester (1941) ▌8,100

North American P-51D Mustang (1944)

North American P-51C Mustang (1943)

Hawker Hurricane I (1940)

Hawker Tempest V (1944)

Boeing B-17F (1942) ▌4,000

Boeing B-17G (1943) ▌6,000

RAF Scampton

London

RAF Biggin Hill

Supermarine Spitfire VC (1942)

Hamburg
Bremen
Berlin

Lockheed P-38G Lightning (1943)

Consolidated B-24J Liberator (1944) ▌5,000

Essen • Dortmund
• Düsseldorf
Cologne

Leipzig
Dresden •

North American B-25J Mitchell ▌4,000

Handley Page Hampden (1940) ▌2,000

Handley Page Halifax (1941) ▌5,800

400 miles

• Frankfurt

Republic P-47D Thunderbolt (1944)

de Havilland Mosquito BIV (1942) ▌2,000

Supermarine Spitfire IA (1940)

• Stuttgart

Bristol Blenheim I (1939) ▌1,000

de Havilland Mosquito NFII (1942)

Handley Page Hampden (1940) ▌4,000

Munich

de Havilland Mosquito FBVI (1943)

Hawker Typhoon (1942)

400 miles
600 miles
600 miles
800 miles
800 miles
1,000 miles
1,000 miles
1,200 miles
1,200 miles

⊢ **BOMBER RANGES**
▌ **BOMB LOADS IN LBS.**
⊢ **FIGHTER RANGES**

But perhaps a still more significant aspect of the North African campaign was that it provided a trial ground for the evolution of the close-support tactics that characterized Allied air operations both in the final stages of the desert war, in Tunisia in 1943, and in the later invasion and conquest of north-western Europe.

Gradually, too, as the pressure on the homeland was eased, the Royal Air Force moved over to the offensive, and the night bombing of Germany began to gather momentum. This was by no means achieved through a mere change of policy. Navigation, for example, at first threatened to be an insuperable problem, and only a minute percentage of the bomb tonnage dropped by the RAF in 1942 and 1943 fell within five miles of its target. However, with the gradual introduction of electronic aids such as H2S, Gee, and Oboe, plus the arrival of the first Pathfinder crews to mark the targets, bombing accuracy improved. From that time, too, the area bombing of targets such as Hamburg, Essen, Cologne and other German industrial centres became a major factor in the RAF's calculations.

H2S was a radar system that scanned the area underneath an aircraft, and thus produced a radar map of the land over which the bomber was flying. Using this device, bomber crews stood a good chance of finding their targets.

Gee was a device using three ground transmitters to lay a grid of varied pulses over Europe. The navigator of a bomber fitted with the correct Gee receiver could measure the pulses and work out from his special map where he was. The device was accurate to six miles at a distance of 400 miles from the farthest receiver.

Oboe was a far more sophisticated device, using the ground radar transmitters and a receiver in the aircraft. By plotting the aircraft's position accurately the first transmitter station, at Dover, could control the aircraft along a circular path towards its destination. The second station, at Cromer, could plot this path and, when the bomber passed over the target, radio instructions to drop the bomb. Range was up to 270 miles.

The Pathfinders were a force of specially selected and trained aircrews under Air Vice-Marshal D. C. T. Bennett. The force was raised, against considerable Bomber Command opposition, to fly ahead of the main bomber force on raids and mark final turning points and the target area. This the crews did with special coloured markers and bombs. Thus the inability of the average bomber crew to find its target with any accuracy at night was to some extent overcome.

But even if the bombing operations of 1942 had been accurate, the aircraft available to RAF Bomber Command were not capable of carrying a sufficient bomb-load far enough into Germany. What was needed was a new sort of machine – a true heavy bomber.

The first to arrive on the scene was the four-engined Short Stirling, which was introduced in August 1940. But, with a bomb-load of 14,000 pounds, a range of only 590 miles and a ceiling of only 19,000 feet, the Stirling was only moderately successful. Even so, its existence ensured that much was learned about operational techniques. Next was the Handley-Page Halifax, the first of which entered service in November 1940. Maximum bomb-load was

First of the new British heavy bombers was the Short Stirling, below, which could carry 14,000 pounds of bombs but had a range of only 590 miles. Next came the Handley-Page Halifax, above, with a range of 1,860 miles for a 5,800-pound bomb load (maximum load was 13,000 pounds). They were followed by the short-lived Avro Manchester, opposite below, which soon gave way to a re-engined version, the famous Lancaster, opposite above, which was Britain's most successful bomber.

13,000 pounds, and with a 5,800-pound load the range was 1,860 miles, a considerable improvement on the Stirling. Defensive armament on both types consisted of eight ·303-inch machine guns – still inadequate against the ever-improving armament of the German night fighters.

Next in the RAF's heavy-bomber inventory came the unsuccessful twin-engined Avro Manchester, which entered service in November 1940 but was soon phased out because its Rolls-Royce Vulture engines were found to be unreliable. Re-engined with four Merlins it became the celebrated Lancaster, which first became available early in 1942. Again, this type had an insufficient defensive armament – eight small machine guns – but offensively it could carry loads up to the massive 22,000-pound Grand Slam 'earthquake' bomb, or a more usual 14,000 pounds over a range of 1,660 miles. The top speeds of the Stirling, Halifax and Lancaster were 270, 285 and 287 mph.

To counter the British night-bomber offensive, the Germans built up a massive night-fighter and anti-aircraft force, the former centred around adapted Bf-110 and Ju-88 aircraft, and the latter around the famous 88-mm gun. Typical of the highly successful Bf-110 night fighters was the G-4, which had an armament of four 20-mm cannon and four 7·9-mm machine guns, a top speed of 342 mph and a range of 1,300 miles. It was equipped with Lichtenstein SN-2 radar. An eminent example of the Ju-88 night fighters was the G-7, which had three 20-mm cannon, three 7·9-mm machine guns and one 13-mm machine gun, a top speed of 389 mph and a range of 1,380 miles. The German night-fighter arm was very efficient, and took a heavy toll of the British night-bomber fleet throughout the campaign.

The best night fighter produced in the war was in all probability the Heinkel 219 Uhu, which entered service in 1943. The A-7 version had an armament of two 30-mm and four 20-mm cannon, a top speed of 416 mph and a range of 1,240 miles. Other notable night fighters of the war were the British Bristol Beaufighter, with an armament of four 20-mm cannon and six ·303-inch machine guns and a top

Focke-Wulf Fw 190A-3

The Focke-Wulf F2 190 fighter and fighter-bomber was Germany's best such aircraft of World War II, the other contender for this position being the Messerschmitt Bf 109. The latter, however, was an older design and reached the end of its development potential before the end of the war, unlike the Fw 190. The Focke-Wulf design was intended as a back-up in the event of the failure of the Messerschmitt fighter, and the first prototype flew on 1 July 1939. Despite initial reservations about its air-cooled radial engine, the design soon showed itself to be an excellent one and and the type was ordered into service.

The aircraft illustrated is a Focke-Wulf Fw 190-3 of 8/JG2 'Richthofen', that is an aircraft of the 8th Staffel or squadron, which was part of the 3rd Gruppe or wing, which was in turn part of the Luftwaffe's 2nd Jagdgeschwader (JG) or fighter group, named 'Richthofen' in honour of the great World War I ace. The vertical bar on the rear fuselage marked all III Gruppe

SPECIFICATIONS

Type		single-seat interceptor fighter
Engine		BMW 801Dg 14-cylinder air-cooled radial, 1,700-hp at take-off
Armament		two 7·92-mm MG17 machine guns with 1,000 rounds per gun, two 2-cm MG151 cannon with 200 rounds per gun, and two 2-cm MGFF cannon with 55 rounds per gun
Speed	391	mph at 20,600 feet
Initial climb rate	2,830	feet per minute
Climb	12	minutes to 26,250 feet
Ceiling	34,775	feet
Range	497	miles
Weight	6,393	lbs (empty)
	8,700	lbs (loaded)
Span	34	feet $5\frac{1}{2}$ inches
Length	28	feet $10\frac{1}{2}$ inches
Height	12	feet $11\frac{1}{2}$ inches

OPPOSITE

FW 190A-3: *major early production model with extra pair of fast-firing 2-cm cannon in the wing roots, and slower-firing guns moved outboard.*

FW 190D-9: *first major 'long-nose' production model, introduced late in 1943; 426 mph; armament reduced to two cannon and two machine guns.*

FW 190F-8: *most important close-support model; it carries 24 5-cm air-to-air missiles, or 14 anti-tank missiles, or various bomb-loads.*

86

aircraft, and red was the colour for the 2nd, 5th and 8th Staffeln. Staffeln *1–3* belonged to I Gruppe, *4–6* to II, and *7–9* to III.

The Fw 190 was introduced into active service slowly, and was not met in combat until August 1941. However, its debut was startling, and the new radial-engined fighter quickly showed itself to be superior to any British aircraft in service. The next major series to follow the A mark was the 190-D, in 1943. This was in fact a radically redesigned version, an inline Junkers Jumo engine replacing the radial BMW 801. The new engine was cowled in the same type of nose as the earlier model, the radiator forming the annular nose of the aircraft; but the Jumo was a longer engine, and thus the fuselage had to be extended. The 'long-nose' D series was eventually developed in the highly-successful Ta 152. Armament of the D series included a 3-cm cannon in the nose. After the D came the F, a development of the A series with additional armour and reduced armament to fulfil the ground-attack role. The G series of fighter-bombers could carry up to 2,200 pounds of bombs.

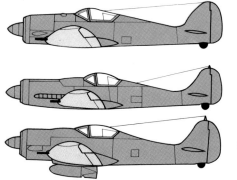

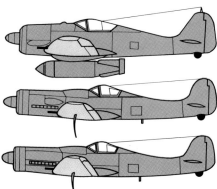

FW 190G-1: *fighter-bomber; bomb-load up to 3,970 pounds; preceded the F series into service; specially strengthened undercarriage for increased loads.*

TA 152C-1: *interceptor fighter; one 3-cm and four 2-cm cannon; 466 mph with methanol-water (MW 50) fuel injection to Daimler-Benz 603LA.*

TA 152H-1: *high-altitude interceptor; span 47 feet 6¾ inches; only two 2-cm cannon; speed 472 mph with nitrous-oxide injection; ceiling 48,560 feet.*

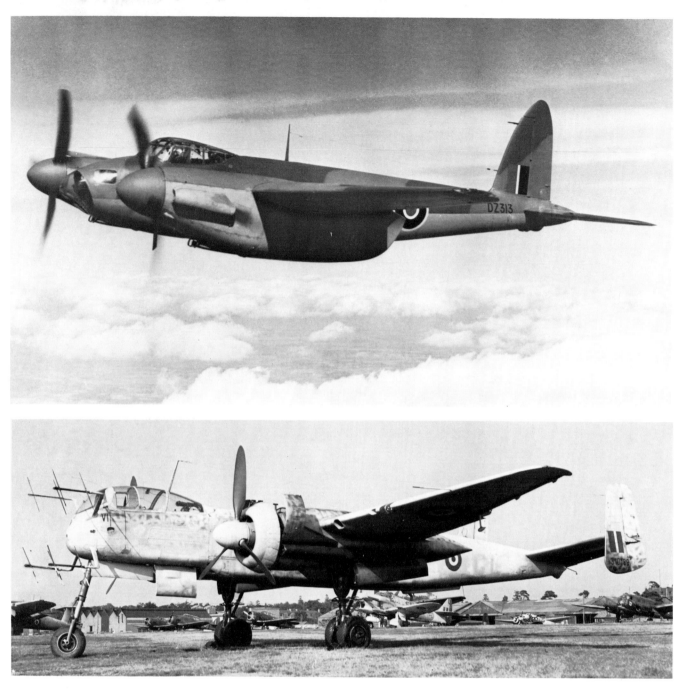

speed of 323 mph; the de Havilland Mosquito NF Mark XII, armed with four 20-mm cannon and four ·303-inch machine guns and with a top speed of 370 mph and a range of 1,860 miles; and the American Northrop P-61 Black Widow, which had an armament of four 20-mm cannon and four ·5-inch machine guns, a top speed of 430 mph and a range of 1,415 miles.

The Beaufighter and the Mosquito also served in other roles. The Beaufighter found its greatest fame as an anti-shipping strike fighter, where its armament of cannon, torpedo and eight rockets gave it phenomenal firepower. The Mosquito, like the Ju-88, was a design of almost limitless possibilities. It was of wooden construction, and served from autumn 1941 as an unarmed bomber, a reconnaissance machine, a fighter-bomber, a night fighter, and as a strike fighter. As a bomber it could outfly almost any German fighter other than the Focke-Wulf Fw-190, even when carrying a 4,000-pound bomb-load, and in its other roles it showed extreme manoeuvrability, considerable load-carrying capacity, and great ruggedness. Powered by two Merlin inlines, the slowest version, the NF Mark II, was still capable of 370 mph, and the fastest, the Bomber Mark XVI, could achieve 415 mph. Truly the Mosquito was one of the world's great aircraft.

With the gradual switch from the strategic defensive of 1940–42 to the offensive of late 1943–44, the RAF needed to develop new types to support land operations. In the field of strike aircraft, two magnificent types were produced, the Hawker Typhoon and the Hawker Tempest. Both were powered by massive inline engines and were very heavy

The war produced a number of fine night fighters on both sides.
OPPOSITE, ABOVE *The de Havilland Mosquito, which also served as a bomber, a strike fighter and as a reconnaissance machine.*
OPPOSITE, BELOW *A captured Heinkel He-219 Uhu with Allied markings.*
ABOVE *The Bristol Beaufighter, another versatile machine that performed equally well as an anti-shipping strike fighter.*
LEFT *The powerful Henschel Hs-129, primarily a ground-attack aircraft, armed with a 75-mm anti-tank gun protruding from a specially designed ventral gondola.*

machines. The Typhoon had a troublesome entry into service as a result of certain structural weaknesses in the tail, and although it failed in its intended role as an interceptor, it proved a very useful ground-attack machine with its four 20-mm cannon and eight 60-pound rockets or two 1,000-pound bombs. It entered service in 1942, and was later joined by the Tempest, which carried the same armament but had a top speed 15 mph higher at 427 mph and a range 550 miles greater at 1,530 miles.

The Germans also produced some good ground-attack aircraft, notably the Henschel Hs-129, armed with a powerful 75-mm anti-tank gun but underpowered, and the G-1 model of the Ju-87, which featured two 37-mm cannon. There were also ground-attack versions of the Ju-88, the P-1 and P-2, mounting a 75-mm gun or two 37-mm cannon

respectively. The ubiquitous Focke Wulf Fw-190 could also operate very effectively as a ground-attack machine, but it was in its true element as a fighter. Introduced in late 1940, the Fw-190 soon acquired a formidable reputation and was in all probability the best conventional fighter produced by the Germans. Early models had four 7·9-mm machine guns, but two of these were soon changed to 20-mm cannon, and then an additional pair of 20-mm cannon was added. Later models had a 30-mm cannon firing through the propeller boss or could carry a single 4,000-pound bomb in the fighter-bomber role. The early A-2 version was capable of 389 mph, but later models reached 426 mph with an inline engine replacing the original radials; the last model, the Ta-152H-1, was capable of 472 mph with nitrous oxide injection.

The Eastern Front

In the field of tactical air power, it was the Russians who ruled supreme at the end of the war. Their Air Force was for the most part obsolescent when Germany invaded the Soviet Union on 22 June 1941 (Operation Barbarossa), and the Russians lost almost all their front-line aircraft. In the short term this was a disastrous blow, but in the long run it had its uses since the Russians could then turn their whole attention to producing the best possible designs for the specific job of supporting the armies on the ground. In the course of the war Russia produced some excellent fighters, such as the Lavochkin LaGG-3, the La-5 and -7, and the Yakovlev Yak-3, -7 and -9. Both series were simple, rugged designs, unsophisticated by Western standards but more than adequate to the task in hand (their German counterparts were the Bf-109 and Fw-190).

OPPOSITE *A Russian Yak-3 fighter and ground attack plane, armed with one 20-mm cannon and two machine guns.*
ABOVE *The LaGG-3; a rugged, all-wood design, she carried one cannon, three machine guns and up to 484 pounds of bombs.*

ABOVE *German aircraft wrecked on a forward airfield near Minsk on the 2nd Byelorussian Front in 1944.*
BELOW *Russian Il-2 assault planes bank towards the target area; agility at low altitudes was a feature of most Soviet fighters.*

The basic design philosophy of the Russians was to update designs as necessary, disturbing production as little as possible. This explains the basic similarities retained in particular series. The La-7 appeared in 1943, and had a top speed of 425 mph. Armament comprised three 20-mm cannon, which proved equal to their task in the type's first battle, fought above the great tank action around Kursk in 1943. The Yak-9 was brought into service in 1945 and had an armament of one 20-mm cannon and two 12·7-mm machine guns, with a top speed of 415 mph in the 7-P variant and a range of 900 miles.

In the ground-attack field, the Russians had the superlative Ilyushin Il-2m3. This was a massive two-seater, the central portion of the machine actually being built of armour plate which rendered it all but immune from ground fire. (Germany's Henschel Hs-129 was designed to a similar requirement but it was underpowered and generally

not a success.) Armed with two 20-mm cannon, three smaller cannon, eight 83-mm rockets and up to 1,325 pounds of bombs, the Il-2m3 could deliver devastating attacks at very low levels. Top speed was 264 mph and range only 372 miles, but the type was designed to absorb punishment and could operate from airfields close up behind the line. It provided invaluable service in the major battles from Stalingrad to Kursk and then during the Russians' two-year drive to Berlin.

Best of the Russian bombers was the Petlyakov Pe-2, a sturdy and agile machine that performed remarkably well in a variety of roles: first and foremost it operated as a conventional light bomber, but it also did valuable duty in the reconnaissance and ground-attack roles. The Pe-2's stablemate in the bitter combat that raged over and beyond the Russian and German front lines was the Tupolev SB-2, a veteran of the Spanish Civil War which was nevertheless fast, handy and could carry a sizeable bomb-load (up to

2,200 pounds). The SB-2 was primarily used as a light/medium bomber on a virtually non-stop programme of raids on enemy positions.

The chief German counterparts of these two machines were the Heinkel He-111, the highly versatile Junkers Ju-88 and the Dornier Do-17 (the 'Flying Pencil'). All of these were of mid-late 1930s vintage, but their reliability at a time when the German war industry found itself under extreme pressure kept them in service for almost the entire war.

OPPOSITE *The urgent scramble to outbuild the enemy, seen at a wartime Russian aircraft factory. After the German invasion of 1941, many munitions factories were evacuated and re-established as far to the east as the Urals.*

TOP *The ANT-42, forerunner of the Petlyakov Pe-8 heavy bomber.*

ABOVE *Petlyakov Pe-2 light bombers, armed with five machine guns and up to 2,200 pounds of bombs.*

Ilyushin Il-2m3

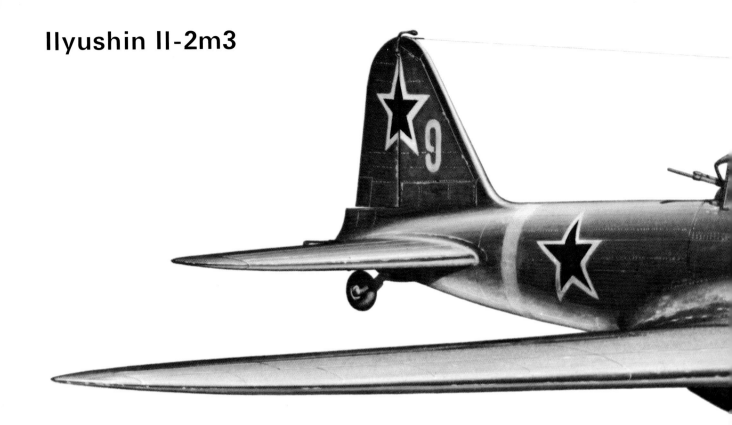

The Ilyushin Il-2 was the Red Air Force's most successful and most celebrated aircraft of World War II. In all, some 35,000 examples of the type were built, making it the most widely produced aircraft of all time. To the world in general the Il-2 is known as the *Shturmovik*, but to the combatants of the Eastern Front it was known differently: *Ilyusha* to the Russians, and *Schwarz Tod* (Black Death) to the Germans.

The task envisaged in the 1930s for the Red Air Force in any future war was that of tactical support for the army, hence the need for a fast, rugged, self-sufficient ground-attack aircraft capable of dealing knock-out blows to enemy tanks, pillboxes and infantry. Several designers produced unsuccessful prototypes, and then in late 1939 Sergei V. Ilyushin completed his CKB-57. The type proved successful after it was given a more powerful engine (1,680-hp AM-38) in place of the original 1,370-hp AM-35, and it was ordered into production as the Il-2 in March 1941. The most notable features of the Il-2 were the raised cockpit enclosure for the pilot and the armoured 'bath' which formed the front part of the fuselage. This was made of armour plate between 5 and 12 mm thick, and protected the engine and cockpit: examination of shot-down *Shturmoviki* usually revealed that this armour bath was intact although the rest of the machine might have been almost totally destroyed.

This first production proved moderately successful in combat, but certain defects were soon brought to the notice of the designers by combat pilots. Chief amongst these were the lack of a second crew member, a gunner, to provide rear defence, and lack of adequate armament to deal with the newer German armoured vehicles. The new requirements were finalized in spring 1942, and soon the Il-2m3 (model 3) appeared. This had a lengthened cockpit enclosure (with the armour bath lengthened also to protect it) to accommodate the rear gunner, and 23-mm VJa cannon in place of the earlier 20-mm Shvak weapons,

the muzzle velocity of which had been found to be too low.

In 1943 the VJa cannon were in turn replaced by 37-mm N-37 (or 11-P-37) cannon, which had far superior armour-piercing capabilities. So armed, the aircraft now became the Il-2m3 (Modified), entering service just in time to render invaluable service against German armour in the Battle of Kursk in July 1943. By this time the Russians were also using 132-mm rockets to replace the earlier 82-mm weapons for attacks on fixed emplacements. These large rockets could carry a hollow-charge warhead that proved absolutely devastating. Other modifications allowed the Il-2 to carry a 21-inch torpedo below the fuselage or a reconnaissance camera in the fuselage behind the gunner. The final development of the basic design was in fact a considerable redesign, and appeared too late to see service in World War II. It was produced as the Il-10.

The Il-2 was at its most effective at low altitude. and many missions were flown at heights of below 200 feet. This meant that Il-2 pilots were often able to obtain complete surprise and attack German armour and emplacements with horizontal fire, very close to right angles with the armour plate—the most effective angle. The best tactic employed by Il-2 pilots was the co-called 'circle of death', in which the aircraft crossed the front to one side of the target and then attacked from the rear, then circled round again, allowing the aircraft behind it in the circle to launch its attack. A dozen aircraft could keep up this tactic of continuous attack for about 30 minutes until all their ammunition was expended. At Kursk 20 minutes of this tactic cost the 9th Panzer Division 70 tanks; another spell of 120 minutes reduced the 3rd Panzer Division by 270 tanks and a further attack lasting 240 minutes destroyed 240 tanks out of the 17th Panzer Division's total of 300. Undoubtedly the Ilyushin Il-2 was a magnificent fighting aircraft. It was also the Red Air Force's safest combat type of World War II.

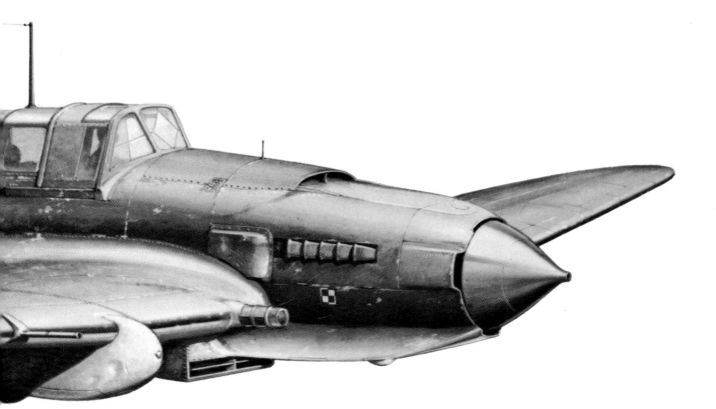

SPECIFICATIONS

Type		two-seat ground-attack aircraft
Engine		Mikulin AM-38F 12-cylinder Vee
		liquid-cooled inline, 1,770-hp at take-off
Armament		two 23-mm VJa cannon, two 7·62-mm
		Shkas machine guns, and one 12·7-mm
		BS machine gun, plus one DAG 10
		grenade launcher and eight 83-mm
		RS 82 or 132-mm RS 132 rockets, or
		1,325 pounds of bombs
Speed	251	mph at 6,560 feet
Ceiling	19,500	feet
Range	372	miles
Weight	9,604	lbs (empty)
	12,136	lbs (loaded)
Span	48	feet 0½ inch
Length	38	feet 0½ inch
Height	11	feet 1½ inches

The Ilyushin Il-2m3 illustrated was a machine of the Assault Regiment of the 1st Polish Mixed Air Division in 1945.

America's War

The country that turned out more aircraft than any other in World War II was the United States. Luckily for them, and for the Allied effort, the Americans did not enter the war in 1939 but in December 1941, after the Japanese attack on Pearl Harbor. This in effect gave them time to improve the the state of their Air Force, which had previously been as unprepared as those of her principal allies.

The US had long been proponents of the theory of strategic bombing, and produced the progenitor of all World War II's heavy four-engined bombers in the Boeing Model-299 bomber of 1935, which was accepted into service by the Americans in 1939 as the B-17 Flying Fortress. This large machine was designed to operate in fleets, delivering massive knock-out blows in daylight precision raids. The heavy defensive armament of each

bomber would, it was confidently expected, interlock to prevent any enemy fighter breaking into the bomber box. As a result of combat experience with the Royal Air Force, the 17E of 1941 became the first really definitive combat model: it introduced a tail turret, a ventral 'ball' turret, increased armour and fuel-tank protection, and the fitting of a uniform machine-gun armament throughout (all ·5-inch guns). This still proved insufficient however, and an additional twin-gun 'chin' turret was added on the final model, the 17G (as the name suggests, it was sited beneath and slightly to the rear of the nose). The B-17's useful bomb-load was somewhere in the region of 8,000 pounds for long-range missions. All production models were powered by variants of the Wright R-1830 Cyclone radial, and the top speed of the early B-17B (291 mph) gradually

OPPOSITE *A B-24D Liberator bomber flying low over the English coast on the 'Biscay Beat' patrol.*
LEFT *B-17 Flying Fortresses over Germany during a mission to bomb Nazi fighter factories in Brunswick.*
BELOW *A Chinese sentry stands guard under the wing of a B-25 Mitchell medium bomber.*

crept up to the 323 mph of the 17C and then down again to 287 mph on the heavily loaded 17G. Range for these three models was 2,400, 2,000 and 2,000 miles respectively, with ceilings at 36,000, 37,000 and 35,600 feet.

The other main heavy bomber of the B-17's vintage was the Consolidated B-24 Liberator, a large and heavy four-engined machine. Deliveries to the USAAF began early in 1941, though earlier consignments had gone to the Royal Air Force. The type went through many modifications, culminating in the B-24J model. This had a defensive armament of ten ·5-inch machine guns, an offensive load of 12,800 pounds, a top speed of 290 mph and a range of 2,100 miles. It performed sterling service in Europe but was really at its best in the Pacific, where its reliability and the services of the automatic pilot were keenly valued.

The third of the United States' heavy bombers was the Boeing B-29 Superfortress, which was used only in the Pacific theatre. Deliveries of this super-bomber began in July 1943 and it proved a remarkably successful design, with exceptional load and range characteristics. Aircraft of this type dropped the atomic bombs on Hiroshima and Nagasaki to end the war against Japan. Powered by four Wright R-3350 radials, the B-29 had a top speed of 358 mph at 25,000 feet, a range of 3,250 miles and a ceiling of 31,850 feet. Stripped of most of its defensive armament, it could carry up to 20,000 pounds of bombs.

The USA also had several very useful medium bombers: the North American B-25 Mitchell, the Martin B-26 Marauder and the Douglas Boston, or Havoc, which was normally used in the attack role under the designation A-20.

The B-25 was a really outstanding design, which entered service in the second half of 1940. The various models carried up to fourteen ·5-inch machine guns and 3,000 pounds of bombs at speeds of about 280 mph over ranges of 1,500 miles. The B-26 entered service in 1941 and was armed with up to eleven ·5-inch machine guns and 4,000 pounds of bombs or a torpedo. Top speed was 283 mph in the G model, and range was 1,100 miles. The A-20 proved eminently suited to the attack role, and had a top speed of 339 mph in the G model, and a range of 1,100 miles.

As far as fighters were concerned, the US Army's main fighter in 1941 was the Curtiss P-40 series. This was an adequate design when it first appeared, but it was obsolescent by the time the US entered the war. It suffered very badly at the hands of the Japanese, its only advantages

being its strength and high diving speed. However, three new fighters soon appeared to take over from the P-40: the Republic P-47 Thunderbolt, the North American P-51 Mustang, and the Lockheed P-38 Lightning.

The P-47 was the biggest single-engined fighter to see service in the war, and was a huge radial-engined monoplane derived from the earlier P-43 Lancer. It was armed with six or eight ·5-inch machine guns, and was later given provision for a massive load of bombs and rockets. Top speed rose from the 412 mph of the B version to the 467 mph of the N, with ranges of over 1,000 miles available with drop tanks. One experimental model even topped 500 mph.

The P-51 was a classic design. Originally suggested by a British mission visiting the United States to buy aircraft, the first P-51 flew in 1940. Powered by an Allison inline, it

OPPOSITE *An American P-38 Lightning fighter, one of several successors to the Curtiss P-40 series.*

TOP *P-47 Thunderbolts of the 10th USAAF fly over hills in northern Burma on a mission against Japanese installations.*

ABOVE *The aggressive if portly shape of the US Navy's Grumman F4F Wildcat fighter; unequal to the Japanese Zeros, it was in time superseded by the Hellcat.*

LEFT *The P-51 Mustang, a classic high-performance fighter-bomber and escort machine.*

did not at first prove very successful, but when re-engined with the Packard-built Merlin its performance was phenomenal: speed rose from 390 mph in the A model to 439 mph in the C, and to 487 mph in the final H model. At the same time range was increased from 450 miles to well over 1,000 with the use of drop tanks. Ceiling also increased from 31,350 feet to 41,900, and then to 42,000 feet. Armament comprised six ·5-inch machine guns plus two 1,000-pound bombs or racks of rockets. Apart from its performance, the P-51 also had superb handling characteristics, and provided the USAAF with its first escort fighter capable of taking Flying Fortresses to Berlin and back.

The third of the USAAF's main fighters was the Lockheed P-38 Lightning, a clean-lined twin-boom design introduced into service in the middle of 1941. Armament comprised four machine guns and one cannon, plus bombs and rockets on later models. The P-38G had a top speed of 400 mph and a range with drop tanks well in excess of 1,000 miles.

The US Navy has its own air force, and its machines need to be discussed separately, in particular because they formed the backbone of American air power in the Pacific. Whereas the USAAF's aircraft, with the exception of the Superfortress, served in both Western and Eastern theatres, the bulk of the US Navy's forces was deployed against Japan in an all-out effort to eliminate Japanese air and sea power.

At the beginning of the war, the main carrier-borne fighter in service was the portly Grumman F4F Wildcat, which entered service in 1940. Although armed with only

Some of the Allied carrier aircraft in World War II.
OPPOSITE *US Devastator torpedo-bombers spread their wings in readiness for take-off.*
OPPOSITE, BELOW *Escort carriers in stormy weather, the fighters lashed to the flight decks.*
LEFT *A US Navy Dauntless dive-bomber in action in the Pacific.*
BELOW *Barracudas and Corsairs on the forecastle of HMS* Illustrious.

four ·5-inch machine guns, the Wildcat was reasonably fast, at 330 mph, and had a good range of some 845 miles; added equipment in the definitive F4F-4 reduced these figures to 318 mph and 770 miles. The type was not quite a match for the Zero of the Imperial Japanese Navy, however, and in late 1942 the Grumman F6F Hellcat began to enter service. This was basically a scaled-up and more powerful version of the Wildcat, and it proved very successful. Armament was six ·5-inch machine guns, top speed 375 mph and range 1,090 miles.

The US Navy started the war with the Douglas TBD-1 Devastator as its standard torpedo bomber, but this was quickly replaced by the more modern Grumman TBF Avenger, which entered service in January 1942. This type turned out to be a robust design, well able to take care of itself in the air. The TBF-1 had a top speed of 271 mph and a range of 1,215 miles.

Also serving in large numbers on US and Allied carriers was the Douglas SBD Dauntless, a tough and accurate dive-bomber which did much to redress the early imbalance of naval forces in favour of the United States. Offensive armament was a 1,000-pound bomb, top speed 262 mph (in the SBD-6 version) and range 1,230 miles.

Finally, in this brief review of the aircraft of the US Navy, we must mention the great Vought F4U Corsair. Armed with six ·5-inch machine guns and 2,000 pounds of bombs or eight rockets, the Corsair was indubitably the best carrier-borne machine of the war, either as a fighter or as a strike aircraft. Capable of 446 mph in the F4U-4 version, it could outfly any Japanese aircraft put up against it.

Other significant maritime aircraft were the Consolidated PBY Catalina flying boat, the Consolidated PB2Y Coronado flying boat, the British Short Sunderland flying boat, and the totally obsolete yet very useful Fairey Swordfish torpedo and reconnaissance aircraft. These did much to defeat the U-boat menace during the war, and even if their part was not necessarily a glamorous one, it was one whose importance can hardly be overestimated.

Inevitably, in turning to Japanese aircraft, we must think of the Mitsubishi A6M Zero, or Zeke. This carrier-borne fighter raised the art of the naval aircraft designer to new heights. It was capable at the height of its importance of besting most of its land-based opponents, and it remained a formidable opponent, although obsolescent, right to the end

The fighting machines of Imperial Japan.
OPPOSITE, TOP *A Kawasaki Ki-61 Hien fighter, nicknamed Tony.*
OPPOSITE, CENTRE *A Kamikaze suicide plane crashes on the flight deck of HMS Illustrious.*
OPPOSITE, BOTTOM *One of the famous A6M Zeros in flight.*
ABOVE LEFT *Japanese aircraft captured by Soviet troops at an airfield in Changchun, north-east China.*
LEFT *A Mitsubishi G4M bomber (Betty) unloads her bombs over Rangoon.*
BELOW LEFT *The Aichi D3A Val dive-bomber; this photo was taken from captured Japanese film.*

of the war. Armed with two 20-mm cannon and two 7·7-mm machine guns, it had considerable firepower – though its protection was inadequate and by the end of the war even small bursts of concentrated ·5-inch machine-gun fire were sufficient to knock it down. The Aichi D3A Val dive-bomber and Nakajima B5N torpedo bomber were worthy companions for the Zero in the opening months of the Pacific war.

On land, the Japanese had several notable designs, including the Kawasaki Ki-61 Hien fighter, the Mitsubishi G-4M bomber, the Nakajima Ki-43 Hayabusa fighter and the Nakajima Ki-84 Hayate fighter. But Japanese design always lagged a little behind the Americans, and this, combined with lack of fuel, severely limited Japanese air activity from the middle of 1943 onwards.

A New Era

Among the machines of World War II were types that presaged a new era in aircraft design – the turbojets. Only three of these saw service in the war: the Messerschmitt Me-262 twin-jet fighter, the Arado Ar-234 Blitz bomber, and the Gloster Meteor fighter.

Research into jet propulsion had been going on since before the war (Germany's first jet aircraft, the Heinkel He-178, had flown before the outbreak of hostilities) but both Germany and Britain placed higher priority on more conventional types until late in the war. The United States was also developing jet aircraft by the end of the war, but in common with British types these were little more than machines based on the piston-engined design philosophy and adapted for jet engines.

First age of the turbojets—and a new rocket type.
RIGHT *The British Gloster Meteor fighter.*
BELOW *The Arado Ar-234 Blitz bomber; the projection above the cockpit is a fairing for the periscope bomb sight and gun sight.*
BOTTOM LEFT *Messerschmitt's Me-163B Komet, a single-seat rocket-propelled interceptor fighter powered by the dangerous Walter bi-fuel liquid rocket unit.*
BOTTOM RIGHT *The Messerschmitt Me-262 twin-jet fighter.*

The Germans, however, had made very considerable advances in the field of aerodynamics, and this led them to adopt the slightly swept wing of the Me-262, while further types, still on the drawing board at the end of the war, were even more advanced. This design material, captured by the Americans and the Russians in 1945, was to prove a revelation, as will be seen in the next chapter. Meanwhile, of the three types actually to see active service, none had a profound effect on the outcome of the war. Also of note was the Messerschmitt Me-163, a swept delta-winged design powered by a highly dangerous rocket engine. Clearly, by 1945 the era of the piston engine was approaching its end.

Chapter Five
The Post-War Years

In the aftermath of World War II, the world's aeronautical manufacturers suffered many of the afflictions that had plagued their predecessors after the end of World War I. The state of the art was advancing rapidly, but post-war economic retrenchment meant that governments had to spend the resources available to them on general re-building, rather than on re-equipping their armed forces.

So radical, however, were the possibilities opened up by the development of the turbojet engine as a means of propulsion, that most of the victorious nations thought that research into jet engines should continue at a high level of priority. The British were the only Allies to have had an operational jet aeroplane in the war, but the Americans had also designed several types; meanwhile, too, with the aid of captured German technical personnel and wartime information from her Allies, the Russians were soon in the race. And the French, somewhat more slowly, built up the

theoretical and experimental background that has made their aerospace industry one of the most formidable in the world today.

As we have noted, Great Britain had an initial advantage in jet aircraft over the United States, and soon after the war she had three types in the air – the wartime Meteor fighter, the new de Havilland Vampire fighter and the English Electric Canberra bomber. Then the Americans' vast aeronautics industry began to catch up with Britain, and although her earliest jets did not prove successful, with the exception of the Lockheed F-80 Shooting Star, by the end of 1946 the first of a new generation, the Republic F-84 Thunderjet, had flown.

It was notable in all these designs that the new jet aircraft were little more advanced than contemporary piston-engined machines: they were, in effect, the piston-engined concept powered by the new jets. But all this began to alter

LEFT *A Yak-15, officially the first Soviet jet fighter, photographed in 1946.*

ABOVE LEFT *The USAF's Lockheed F-80 Shooting Star, America's first successful jet fighter.*
ABOVE *The British Vampire fighter, a World War II design still much in evidence at the time of the Korean War (1950–53).*
LEFT *Another British jet of the post-war period, the English Electric P-1 Canberra bomber.*

as the results of German wartime research into high-speed aerodynamics, captured in large quantities by the Allies at the end of the war, began to filter through into the latest designs. Most important among the Germans' researches had been the work into the problem of compressibility and how the worst effects of this might be avoided or overcome.

This problem is basically a simple one: as the aircraft approaches the speed of sound, the air displaced by the aircraft is compressed into a series of high-pressure waves that stream back in a cone from the nose of the machine. As these hit the wing, they cause the airflow over that part of the aircraft to break up, resulting in an increase of drag; they also set up extreme buffeting conditions, with harmful effects to the structure of the wing. The Germans found that if they swept back the wing, this delayed the onset of compressibility problems and allowed higher subsonic speeds to be attained. Soon the results of their findings had been checked and assimilated into American design philosophy, and a new batch of swept-wing aircraft began to take shape on the drawing boards.

Despite these advances, the mainstays of most of the world's air forces in the period up to the beginning of the Korean War (1950–53) remained the types flown in or designed during World War II. In Britain they were the Meteor, Vampire, Tempest, Spitfire and the Lincoln bomber; in the United States the Thunderjet, Shooting Star, Mustang, Superfortress, and the mighty Convair B-36 six-engined pusher bomber; and in the Soviet Union there was an assortment of wartime types with a hybrid mixture of machines boosted by jets or rockets.

The Korean War itself acted as a great spur to progress. After some initial reverses the Americans (under the aegis of the United Nations) fought back with great vigour and were soon thinking that they would be able to end the war without much further delay. How mistaken they were, for the Communist Chinese (who had latterly ousted the last of

The F-84F Thunderstreak fighter and fighter-bomber, in effect the F-84 Thunderjet transformed with a swept-wing layout.

Now a museum piece: a Soviet MiG-15 jet fighter on display at the Monino Aeronautical Museum.

A partner to the famous MiG-15 in the early days of the jet fighter—the Soviet La-15.

TOP *The giant Convair B-36 bomber, a six-engined pusher type in service in the early 1950s.*
ABOVE *The North American F-86A Sabre fighter, a strong swept-wing machine that was built as a counter to the Russian MiG designs.*

Chiang Kai-shek's Nationalists from mainland China) and the Russians started to aid the North Koreans. Here not the least of the Americans' worries was the appearance of some fast and well-armed Russian jet fighters – the Mikoyan-Gurevich MiG-15s. The Russians had produced the type in great secrecy, and the Western Alliance was considerably dismayed to see how much progress they had made in terms of swept-wing design. But the antidote was not long in arriving.

This was the superlative North American F-86 Sabre, a clean-lined, sturdy, swept-wing fighter that was to prove one of the classic combat aircraft of all time. Derived directly from German researches, it was in every way superior to the MiG-15, although it was still armed only with six ·5-inch machine guns. At much the same time, the F-84 underwent major surgery and emerged as the F-84F Thunderstreak, with swept wings and an excellent all-round performance in both the fighter and fighter-bomber roles. A later version, the RF-84F Thunderflash reconnaissance machine, was equally successful and was sold in considerable numbers to America's NATO allies, as were the earlier models.

But the Russians had not been standing still, and in 1953 an updated version of the MiG-15, the MiG-17, appeared. This was similar to the earlier MiG-15, with some aerodynamic refinements. Also flown in the same year was the prototype MiG-19: this was to enter service as the Soviet Union's first supersonic fighter, having a top speed of Mach 1·3. The Americans, working on the same principle, had in the meantime redesigned the Sabre with an increased sweep on the wings and improved aerodynamics to produce their first supersonic fighter, the F-100 Super Sabre.

While the traditional American fighter manufacturers were continuing to press ahead with their chosen types, the major US bomber manufacturer, Boeing, had also turned to jet aircraft. First to appear was the B-47 Stratojet, a clean design with the unusual feature of a bicycle-type undercarriage under the fuselage and outriggers under the inboard engine nacelles to provide added balance. Speed was over 600 mph and range in the order of 4,000 miles, and the type began to enter service in 1951. Soon after this another new Boeing design, the B-52 Stratofortress, appeared. This was similar to the B-47 in appearance but considerably larger, having a span of 185 feet compared with 116 feet, and powered by eight engines instead of six. Deliveries to the US Air Force started in 1955, and since that time the huge B-52 has been the most important type in America's strategic bomber fleet. Needless to say, considerable development has taken place, and although performance remains unaltered (600+ mph and a range in excess of 10,000 miles), its bomb-load has been increased to up to 75,000 pounds, and a considerable array of missiles can be carried for decoy purposes or stand-off bombing. The B-52's multi-purpose electronic equipment has also been refined virtually beyond recognition.

ABOVE *Two F-100 Super Sabres, the USA's first supersonic fighter, and a Super Sabre pilot, equipped for the pressures and g-forces of flying faster than sound.*
FAR LEFT *The Soviet Union's first supersonic fighter, the MiG-19.*
LEFT *The B-47 Stratojet, first of the USA's jet-powered strategic bombers.*

In Europe, the aircraft designed in the early 1950s were not as ambitious as the American machines. Britain's standard fighters, the Meteor and Vampire, were gradually phased out in favour of the newer Hawker Hunter, which soon showed itself to be an excellent and versatile machine in the fighter, ground-attack and reconnaissance roles. The Hunter entered service in 1954, and is still used in large numbers by several European, Middle Eastern and South American countries. At the same time, the first of Britain's nuclear bombers, the Vickers Valiant, was about to enter service. In lieu of an atomic weapon, a maximum of 10,000 pounds of bombs could be carried, a paltry amount compared with the wartime Lancaster (up to 22,000 pounds), let alone the B-52. The Valiant was joined in 1956 by the Avro Vulcan, a massive delta-wing design, which could carry 21,000 pounds of bombs at a high subsonic speed. The

the same time the allweather Sud-Ouest Vautour made its appearance. With the exception of the Mystère, which was transonic, these French aircraft were subsonic, but soon a remarkable supersonic type was to enter upon the scene.

third of Britain's 'V' bombers, the Handley-Page Victor, entered service in 1958. This last was notable for its crescent-shaped wing planform and a design that permitted it to be pushed through the sound barrier in a shallow dive.

By the mid-1950s the French aeronautical industry had recovered from its hard wartime years, and several good designs were either on the drawing boards or already in the air. The post-war Dassault Ouragan fighter was in service and proving a useful machine, and soon after this an up-dated version, the Mystère, entered production. At much

TOP *The Vickers Valiant, first of Britain's nuclear bombers whose maximum bomb capacity in lieu of an atomic weapon was a mere 10,000 pounds.*
ABOVE *The Handley-Page Victor, with its distinctive crescent-shaped wing planform; it entered service in 1958.*

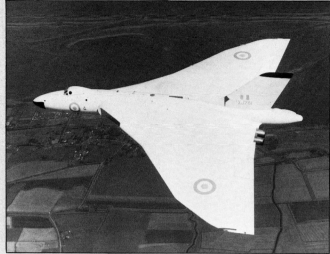

This was the Dassault Mirage, which first appeared in 1955 and soon exceeded the speed of sound. One of the most successful military machines in history, it remains in service today in considerable numbers throughout the world. More important from a design point of view, the Mirage has proved so successful that it has appeared in swept-wing, delta and variable-geometry forms, and also in a scaled-up version, the Mirage IV, which is a nuclear bomber rather than a fighter – as the Mirage was originally conceived.

Britain started development of a supersonic fighter in the 1940s. This was the English Electric Lightning, a squat and powerful design that entered service in 1960 after a protracted development period. The type has since proved successful, and is being exported for service in the interceptor and ground-attack roles.

In Russia, considerable experimental work was undertaken in the 1950s, but the types to enter service were relatively few. The Sukhoi Su-7 and -9 entered service in the late 1950s and are close-support and fighter types respectively. Taking over from the MiG-19 in the late

1950s, the MiG-21 fighter appeared for the first time in 1956, and has been exported extensively within the Warsaw Pact and to Russia's allies in the Middle East and in India. At present the Mach 3 MiG-23 is entering service. This is faster than any of the American machines at present in combat service.

One of the most heated controversies to have occurred in air circles since the end of World War II is the question of the manned strategic bomber. With the development first of the A-bomb, and then of the H-bomb, air power at last

TOP LEFT *A formation of Hawker Hunters, the versatile fighter, ground-attack and reconnaissance machine that came to replace Britain's earlier standard fighters, the Meteor and Vampire.*
TOP RIGHT *No. 2 of Britain's 'V' bombers, the huge delta-wing Avro Vulcan, which entered service in 1956.*

Boeing B-52H Stratofortress

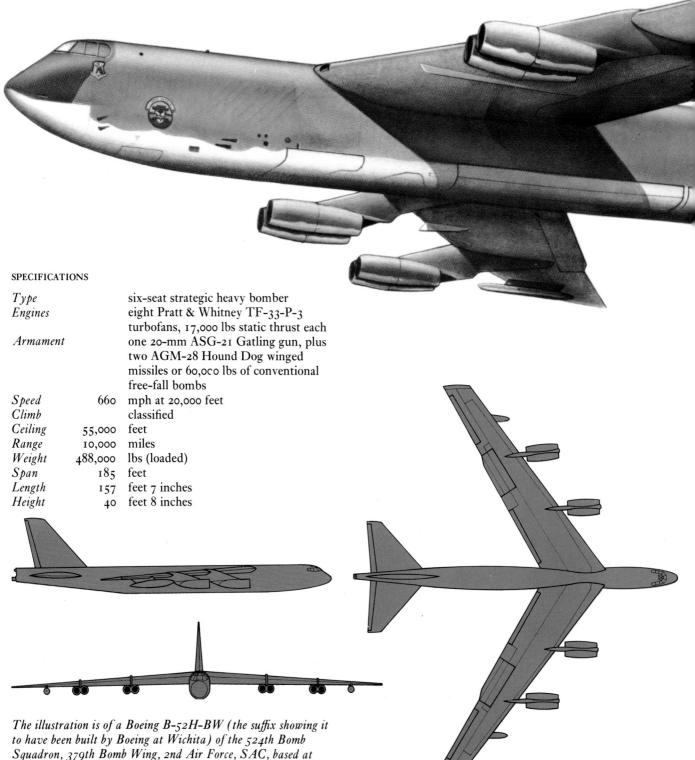

SPECIFICATIONS

Type		six-seat strategic heavy bomber
Engines		eight Pratt & Whitney TF-33-P-3
		turbofans, 17,000 lbs static thrust each
Armament		one 20-mm ASG-21 Gatling gun, plus
		two AGM-28 Hound Dog winged
		missiles or 60,0co lbs of conventional
		free-fall bombs
Speed	660	mph at 20,000 feet
Climb		classified
Ceiling	55,000	feet
Range	10,000	miles
Weight	488,000	lbs (loaded)
Span	185	feet
Length	157	feet 7 inches
Height	40	feet 8 inches

The illustration is of a Boeing B-52H-BW (the suffix showing it to have been built by Boeing at Wichita) of the 524th Bomb Squadron, 379th Bomb Wing, 2nd Air Force, SAC, based at Wurtsmith Air Force Base in Michigan.

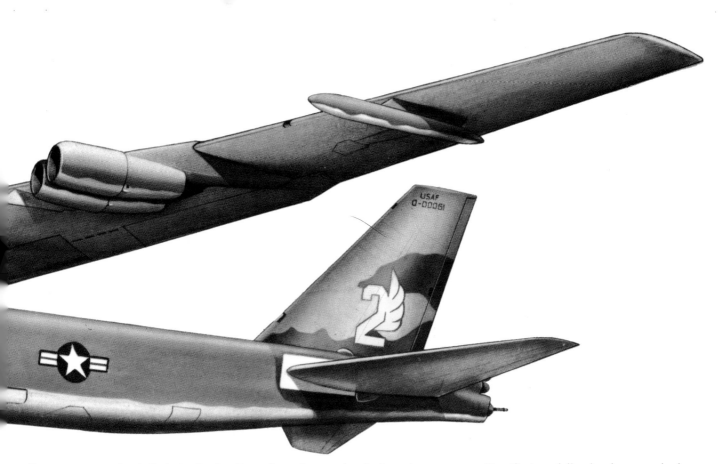

Contrary to popular belief, the Boeing B-52 Stratofortress is not a scaled-up version of the same company's B-47 Stratojet. The design is in fact derived from April 1945 studies for a turboprop-powered long-range bomber to be produced at the same time as the B-47. This originally had straight wings, but soon a 20° sweep was adopted. In July 1948 the USAF ordered two prototype XB-52 aircraft, with turboprop engines, but in an effort to procure a better machine, the turboprop concept was abandoned at the end of the year in favour of a pure jet with eight engines in four underwing pods and wings with 35° of sweep. Although the XB-52 was completed in November 1951, it did not fly until October 1952. It was preceded into the air by the pre-production YB-52 in April.

One of the chief features of the B-52 design is the thin, flexible wing that droops when the aircraft is on the ground, but shows marked dihedral when it is supporting the bomber in the air. As in the B-47, the two main undercarriage members are in the fuselage, outriggers under the wings balancing the aircraft on the ground.

The B-52 was ordered into production in February 1951, and the first production B-52A flew in August 1954. This differed from the XB and YB-52 principally in having the two pilots seated side-by-side in a new cockpit instead of in tandem as in the original design. Development work meant that the first bomber was not delivered to the Strategic Air Command (SAC) until the end of 1957. Better operational equipment was introduced on the B-52B and RB-52B, a reconnaissance version, which first flew in January 1955, deliveries to SAC commencing in June of the same year. On 21 May 1956 a B-52 dropped the first air-dropped hydrogen bomb over Bikini atoll in the Pacific.

The B-52C, which had the same multi-mission capability as the B-52B, flew for the first time in March 1956. This version had larger underwing fuel tanks and increased gross weights. Deliveries began in June 1956. At the same time, the B-52D was in production. The first of these had in fact flown ten days

before the prototype B-52C, but deliveries began only in December. The B-52D was intended only for long-range bombing, and 170 in all were built.

The first example of the next model, the B-52E, flew in October 1957, and had improved bombing, navigation and electronics systems. Deliveries of the 100 produced began in July 1957. The B-52F, which had more powerful engines, first flew in May 1958, and the first of 89 was delivered in June 1958.

The B-52G marked a fairly radical departure from earlier models: fuel tanks in the wing were introduced, the tail gunner was moved up the fuselage to a position near the electronics countermeasures operator, and the fin and rudder were shortened and widened in chord. The first flew in October 1958, and deliveries of the 193 built commenced in February 1959. The B-52G also had the capability of carrying two Hound Dog stand-off missiles, one under each wing.

Final version of the B-52 design is the B-52H, which is powered by turbofan engines, and has improved range and all-up weights. The quadruple ·5-inch rear gun armament is replaced by a single 20-mm multi-barrel 'Gatling gun' fixture. The first B-52H flew in March 1961, and the last of the 102 built was delivered in October 1963.

A total of 744 B-52s was built, the last two versions being able to carry ADM-20 Quail decoy missiles and AGM-69A short-range attack missiles. Up to 20 of these Mach 3 missiles can be carried by the B-52H, six on each of two underwing pylons and eight in a rotary launcher in the bomb bay.

B-52 bombers have not been sold by the United States to any other nations, and have been used in combat only over Indo-China. In this theatre the USAF has used the Stratofortress extensively over Vietnam and Cambodia as a conventional weapons launcher, operating from major bases in Thailand and Guam and bombing from altitude using special ground-scanning radar. The question of a B-52 successor is at present under close scrutiny in the United States.

had a weapon of truly grand strategic capabilities. Initially, only manned bombers could deliver these weapons, and so there was little dissension when the B-36, B-47 and B-52 bombers were built. But the advent of the guided ballistic missile seemed to presage a complete change: delivery systems such as the Atlas, Titan, Minuteman, and submarine-launched Polaris and Poseidon were thought to be capable of supplanting the bomb entirely. However, the development of anti-missile systems has once again put the bomber back into court. For the bomber, unlike the missile, can alter course radically in the light of tactical developments; it can bomb from high and low altitudes, both subsonically and supersonically, and it can bomb a different target if the last-minute situation warrants it. And so it

McDonnell Douglas F-4 Phantom II

SPECIFICATIONS (F-4B)

Type		two-seat interceptor and attack aircraft
Engines		two General Electric J79-GE-8 turbojets, 17,000 lbs thrust each with afterburning
Armament		six Raytheon Sparrow III, or 4 Sparrow III and 4 General Electric Sidewinder I air-to-air missiles, plus up to 16,000 lbs of external stores. These can be made up of a mixture of 250-, 500-, 750-, or 1,000-lb bombs, nuclear weapons, rocket launchers, landmines, napalm bombs, chemical warfare bombs, leaflet bombs, and sometimes GAM-83A Bullpup missiles and 20-mm Vulpod or 7·62-mm Minipod gun packs
Speed	1,548	mph at 48,000 feet (Mach 2·4)
Initial climb rate	28,000	feet per minute
Ceiling	71,000	feet
Combat radius	900	miles
Ferry range	2,300	miles
Weight	28,000	lbs (empty)
	56,000	lbs (loaded)
Span	38	feet $4\frac{7}{8}$ inches
Length	58	feet $3\frac{1}{8}$ inches
Height	16	feet 3 inches

F-4 PHANTOM II MARKS

F-4A: 23 prototypes and 24 training aircraft for US Navy.
F-4B: production ship-board fighter and attack aircraft for the US Navy and US Marine Corps.
RF-4B: unarmed reconnaissance variant for US Marine Corps.
F-4C: air superiority and close support fighter for the USAF.
RF-4C: unarmed reconnaissance variant for USAF.
F-4D: USAF fighter with improved weapons system. Also ordered by Iran.
F-4E: USAF fighter with integral cannon armament. Also ordered by Japan and Israel.
RF-4E: reconnaissance variant of F-4E. Ordered by the West German Air Force or Luftwaffe.
F-4G: experimental adaptation of F-4B for automatic deck-landing trials.
F-4J: improved US Navy and Marine Corps combat type.
F-4K: Spey-engined version of F-4J for Royal Navy.
F-4M: RAF fighter-bomber/reconnaissance version of F-4K.

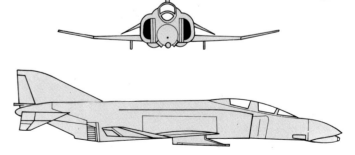

TOP *A US Navy F-4B of the VF-114 Fighter Squadron comes in to land. Note the number of pylon-mounted stores still carried, the arrester hook, and the drooped leading edges and flaps.*

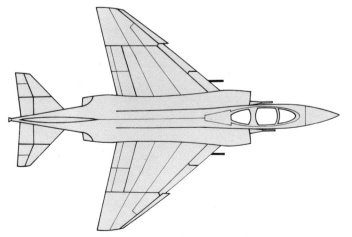

ABOVE AND LEFT *Three views of the Phantom. Note the massive fuselage, 'droop snoot' nose, anhedral tailplane and dihedral only on the outer panels of the wings.*

The McDonnell Douglas F-4 Phantom II can justly be claimed to be the best combat aircraft to have served with the air forces of the Western world since 1945. Although more advanced types will gradually replace the Phantom from 1975 onwards, this versatile machine will still continue to contribute greatly to the attack and defence capability of the West for some time to come.

The Phantom I of 1946 was the US Navy's first operational jet aircraft, and the development of the Phantom II can be traced from its earlier namesake via the F-2H Banshee, the F-3H Demon, and the USAF's F-101 Voodoo. On their own initiative, McDonnell started design work on a new carrier-borne fighter in 1953. By the end of 1954 the Navy had decided that it needed a larger, faster type than had originally been envisaged, and McDonnell redesigned their F-3H-G idea so that by August 1956 construction of the XF-4H-1 prototype Phantom II could begin; it was completed in April 1958 and proved immediately successful. Squadron service began in February 1961.

seems likely that a new generation of heavy bombers will be developed by both the Superpowers.

Certainly Russia has become increasingly conscious since 1945 of her lack of an effective strategic bomber force, and several enormous machines have been produced. Principal amongst these are the Myasishchev Mya-4, which is capable of delivering a 10,000-pound bomb-load over a range of 7,000 miles, the Tupolev Tu-16 medium bomber, the Tu-20 turboprop-driven heavy bomber and long-range reconnaissance machine, the Mach 1·5 Tu-22 and the later Mach 1·5 Tupolev 'Fiddler', as it is codenamed by NATO.

In the 1960s the United States produced a variety of supersonic types, ranging from the not-very-successful Convair B-58 Hustler supersonic bomber and the General Dynamics F-111 variable-geometry fighter and long-range supersonic bomber via the US Air Force's Lockheed F-104 Starfighter, its Convair F-106 Delta Dart interceptors and

Republic F-105 fighter and fighter-bomber to the magnificent McDonnell F-4 Phantom series. This is probably the most successful aircraft ever built for the military, and it has served in the fighter, fighter-bomber, reconnaissance and bomber roles, as well as being able to undertake strike and ground-attack missions. In the Arab-Israeli War of 1973 it was through her Phantoms that Israel eventually achieved air superiority – though she suffered considerable losses from Egypt's Russian-built surface-to-air missiles in the process.

The states of Western Europe, no longer able to match either of the Superpowers, have in recent years opted for the all-purpose, internationally designed and produced aircraft. This has led to the development of such types as the SEPECAT Jaguar trainer, fighter and strike aircraft, and the Multi-Role Combat Aircraft design (MRCA) which is currently under construction by a European consortium.

FAR LEFT, ABOVE *An Egyptian SAM-2 missile captured by Israeli forces on the west bank of the Suez Canal. These surface-to-air missiles accounted for a high proportion of Israeli aircraft in the 1973 war.*

ABOVE *Two American ICBMs, the Titan and Minuteman.*

LEFT *A US Minuteman prototype on its transporter. Despite the power of the ICBMs, the bomber seems likely to hold its own for many years to come, largely because it is more flexible and can react quickly to changes in the tactical situation.*

Helicopters

LEFT *A Chinook helicopter brings supplies and reinforcements to US troops under fire on a hill in South Vietnam.*
ABOVE *The Autogyro, a forerunner of the helicopter idea that was finally perfected by Juan de la Cierva, a Spaniard, and the Russian designer Igor Sikorsky.*
TOP *A British Army Sioux helicopter.*

The helicopter emerged as a practicable military vehicle in the closing stages of World War II, and has grown to a considerable, if disputed, prominence in the last 25 years. Its first widespread use in war occurred in the Korean conflict, where the Americans made considerable use of its then unique vertical take-off and landing and hovering characteristics for observation and casualty evacuation purposes. Since then the type has continued to give valuable service in these two roles, and also as a commando carrier. In this role the Israelis have been the helicopter's chief exponents, using it profitably in 1956, 1967 and 1973.

The Americans, however, have attempted to turn the helicopter into a fighting machine, fitting it with rockets, flexible machine guns and even machine-gun turrets. The most notable of these machines is the Bell Huey Cobra, of which more than 16,000 have been built. But it seems that such a machine can only operate within a tolerable loss limit when the user has complete air superiority, and when the ground forces attacked have no sophisticated anti-aircraft defences. In fact, the American helicopter forces suffered very heavy casualties to ground fire in Vietnam. Thus the future of the helicopter as a strike aircraft is now much in doubt, although poorer countries may be attracted to the idea by the relative cheapness of the helicopter compared with even the least sophisticated conventional aircraft.

Royal Navy helicopters display their lifting powers at the Farnborough Air Show. This is one aspect—the 'passive' side—of the helicopter's military potential, i.e. as a troop and supplies carrier and as a battlefield observer.

On this page are two examples of the fighting helicopter. ABOVE *The British missile-armed Scout machine.*

BELOW *The US Bell HueyCobra, which embodies the helicopter-gunship concept; over 16,000 have been built.*

The Years Ahead

What can the future be expected to bring? Will the Superpowers continue to build considerable numbers of sophisticated and basically one-purpose aircraft, or will they too be forced by the sheer economics of special metals and expensive electronics to turn to the European idea of multi-purpose machines like the MRCA or the cheaper but nonetheless efficient types such as the radical Hawker Siddeley Harrier vertical take-off and landing aircraft?

It is a difficult, if not impossible, question to answer. It is clear, however, that the missile, in aircraft use, is not altogether invincible, and that for some time to come great reliance will still have to be placed on manned aircraft and helicopters armed with guns as well as missiles, and capable of outflying as well as out-thinking their opponents' onboard computers.

ABOVE *First of the MRCA prototypes; the versatility of this low-cost aircraft is described in the diagram opposite.*

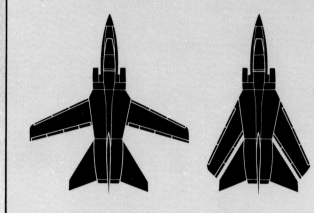

The European MRCA (Multi Role Combat Aircraft) is designed to fulfil five major roles: close air support; interdictor and naval strike; reconnaissance; air superiority, and interception. The MRCA's variable-geometry wing makes it especially versatile: the swept wing ensures a low gust response, giving high speed at low levels during the weapons delivery phase; while the extended wing is used for V/STOL. Some 800 aircraft are planned for service with Britain, Italy and West Germany.

BELOW *Harriers on exercise in Germany. As one machine makes a vertical landing, another is towed to a camouflaged position.*

DATA SECTION
1: Details of Important Aircraft

US Wright Flyer A (1908)

Type		two-seat reconnaissance machine
Engine		Wright 4-cylinder water-cooled inline, 30-hp
Armament		none
Speed	44	mph
Climb	?	
Ceiling	?	
Range	90	miles
Weight	740	lbs (empty)
	1,200	lbs (loaded)
Span	36	feet 6 inches
Length	28	feet 11 inches
Height	8	feet 1 inch

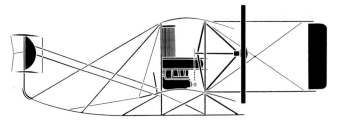

The Military Flyer tested in 1908 and 1909 was an adaptation of the basic Flyer A, and after acceptance became Signal Corps No. 1. Data are for this machine.

French Morane-Saulnier Type N (1913)

Type		single-seat fighter
Engine		Le Rhône 9C 9-cylinder air-cooled rotary, 80-hp
Armament		one fixed 8-mm Hotchkiss machine gun
Speed	90	mph at sea level
Climb	10	minutes to 6,560 feet
Ceiling	13,125	feet
Endurance	1½	hours
Weight	633	lbs (empty)
	976	lbs (loaded)
Span	26	feet 8¾ inches
Length	19	feet 1½ inches
Height	7	feet 4½ inches

The Morane-Saulnier N, a pleasing and well-streamlined monoplane, entered service with the French air force in 1914.

British Royal Aircraft Factory BE 2b (1913)

Type		two-seat reconnaissance machine
Engine		Renault 8-cylinder water-cooled inline, 70-hp
Armament		miscellaneous small arms
Speed	70	mph at sea level
Climb	35	minutes to 7,000 feet
Ceiling	10,000	feet
Endurance	3	hours
Weight	1,274	lbs (empty)
	1,600	lbs (loaded)
Span	35	feet 0½ inch
Length	29	feet 6½ inches
Height	10	feet 2 inches

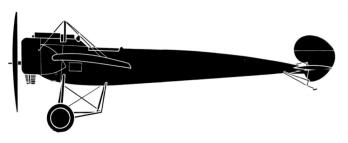

The BE 2b was the first British type to enter quantity production for the RFC.

German Fokker E-III (1915)

Type		single-seat fighter
Engine		Iberursel U-I 9-cylinder air-cooled rotary, 100-hp
Armament		one fixed 7·92-mm Spandau machine gun
Speed	87½	mph at sea level
Climb	30	minutes to 9,840 feet
Ceiling	11,500	feet
Endurance	1½	hours
Weight	878	lbs (empty)
	1,342	lbs (loaded)
Span	31	feet 2¾ inches
Length	23	feet 7½ inches
Height	7	feet 10½ inches

The Fokker E-III was the major production variant of the Fokker *Eindekker* type, the world's first true fighter.

British Handley Page 0/100 (1915)

Type		three-seat heavy bomber
Engines		two Rolls-Royce Eagle II 8-cylinder water-cooled inlines, 266-hp each
Armament		three to five flexible ·303-inch Lewis guns, plus up to 2,000 lbs of bombs
Speed	85	mph at sea level
Climb	15+	minutes to 5,000 feet
Ceiling	7,000	feet
Range	700	miles
Weight	8,300	lbs (empty)
	14,000	lbs (loaded)
Span	100	feet
Length	62	feet 10¼ inches
Height	22	feet

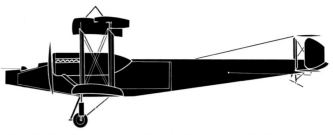

The Handley Page 0/100 was the world's first true night bomber, and originated from an Admiralty request for a 'bloody paralyser' of a bomber. Only 46 examples of the type were built before production was switched to the improved 0/400 with better engines.

British Sopwith 1½-Strutter (1915)

Type		two-seat bomber or reconnaissance machine, or single-seat fighter or bomber
Engine		one Clerget 9B 9-cylinder air-cooled rotary, 130-lb
Armament		one fixed ·303-inch Vickers gun and one flexible ·303-inch Lewis gun, plus up to 136 lbs of bombs
Speed	100	mph at 6,500 feet
Climb	17	minutes 50 seconds to 10,000 feet
Ceiling	15,500	feet
Endurance	3¾	hours
Weight	1,305	lbs (empty)
	2,150	lbs (loaded)
Span	33	feet 6 inches
Length	25	feet 3 inches
Height	10	feet 3 inches

The Sopwith 1½-Strutter, so nicknamed for the whole strut bracing the outer portions of the wings and the 'half' cabane struts supporting the upper wing, was one of Britain's best machines.

German Albatros D-III (1916)

Type		single-seat fighter
Engine		Mercedes D-IIIa 6-cylinder water-cooled inline, 160-hp
Armament		two fixed 7·92-mm Spandau machine guns
Speed	109	mph at sea level
Climb	12	minutes 1 second to 9,840 feet
Ceiling	18,050	feet
Endurance	2	hours
Weight	1,454	lbs (empty)
	1,949	lbs (loaded)
Span	29	feet 8¼ inches
Length	24	feet 0¾ inch
Height	9	feet 9¼ inches

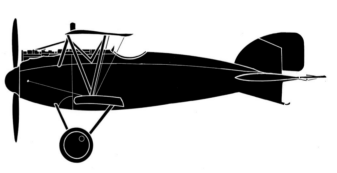

The Albatros D-III was primarily responsible for German air superiority in the early months of 1917.

French Breguet 14B.2 (1916)

Type		two-seat bomber and reconnaissance machine
Engine		Renault 12Fcx 12-cylinder water-cooled inline, 300-hp
Armament		one fixed ·303-inch Vickers gun and two or three flexible ·303-inch Lewis guns, plus up to 560 lbs of bombs
Speed	110	mph at 6,560 feet
Climb	16	minutes 30 seconds to 9,840 feet
Ceiling	19,000	feet
Endurance	2¾	hours
Weight	2,283	lbs (empty)
	3,892	lbs (loaded)
Span	47	feet 1¼ inches
Length	29	feet 1¼ inches
Height	10	feet 10 inches

The Breguet 14 was undoubtedly France's best light bomber of World War I, and began to enter service in September 1917. It had an excellent defensive armament.

British de Havilland 4 (1916)

Type		two-seat bomber
Engine		Rolls-Royce Eagle VIII 8-cylinder water-cooled inline, 375-hp
Armament		one or two fixed ·303-inch Vickers guns and one or two ·303-inch flexible Lewis guns, plus up to 460 lbs of bombs
Speed	143	mph at sea level
Climb	9	minutes to 10,000 feet
Ceiling	22,000	feet
Range	435	miles
Weight	2,387	lbs (empty)
	3,472	lbs (loaded)
Span	42	feet 4¾ inches
Length	30	feet 8 inches
Height	10	feet

The de Havilland 4 was the best light bomber of the war, and served with the American as well as the British air force. Its one failing was the separation of the pilot and the observer, a fault rectified in the otherwise inferior de Havilland 9.

French Nieuport 17 (1916)

Type		single-seat fighter
Engine		Le Rhône 9-cylinder air-cooled rotary, 110-hp
Armament		one .303-inch Vickers or Lewis machine gun
Speed	110	mph at 6,560 feet
Climb	9	minutes to 10,000 feet
Ceiling	17,400	feet
Endurance	2	hours
Weight	825	lbs (empty)
	1,246	lbs (loaded)
Span	26	feet 11¾ inches
Length	18	feet 10 inches
Height	7	feet 7¾ inches

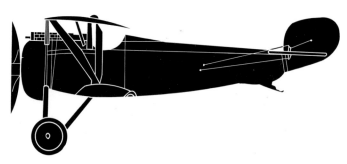

The Nieuport 17 was the best of the company's sesquiplane fighters.

French Spad S.7 (1916)

Type		single-seat fighter
Engine		Hispano-Suiza 8Ac 8-cylinder water-cooled inline, 175-hp
Armament		one fixed ·303-inch Vickers gun
Speed	119	mph at 6,560 feet
Climb	11	minutes 30 seconds to 9,840 feet
Ceiling	18,000	feet
Endurance	2¼	hours
Weight	1,100	lbs (empty)
	1,550	lbs (loaded)
Span	25	feet 8 inches
Length	20	feet 3½ inches
Height	7	feet

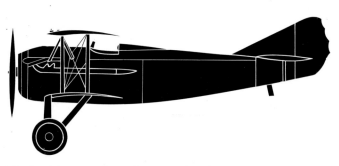

The Spad S.7 was a fast and very sturdy fighter, and was an excellent gun platform.

Italian Ansaldo SVA-5 (1917)

Type		single-seat reconnaissance and bomber machine
Engine		SPA Type 6A 6-cylinder water-cooled inline, 220-hp
Armament		two fixed ·303-inch Vickers guns
Speed	143	mph at sea level
Climb	10	minutes to 9,840 feet
Ceiling	22,000	feet
Endurance	4	hours
Weight	1,507	lbs (empty)
	2,090	lbs (loaded)
Span	29	feet 10¼ inches
Length	26	feet 7 inches
Height	10	feet 6 inches

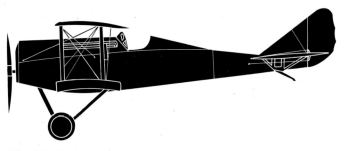

The Ansaldo SVA-5, although designed as a fighter, lacked the manoeuvrability vital for this function in World War I, and found its *métier* as a long-range strategic reconnaissance machine.

German Fokker D-VII (1917)

Type.		single-seat fighter
Engine		BMW IIIa 6-cylinder water-cooled inline, 185 mph
Armament		two fixed 7·92-mm Spandau machine guns
Speed	124	mph at sea level
Climb	8	minutes 30 seconds to 9,840 feet
Ceiling	22,900	feet
Endurance	1½	hours
Weight	1,513	lbs (empty)
	1,993	lbs (loaded)
Span	29	feet 3½ inches
Length	22	feet 9¾ inches
Height	9	feet 2 inches

The Fokker D-VII was undoubtedly Germany's best fighter of World War I, and may have been the equal of the British Sopwith Camel.

German Hannover CL-IIIa (1917)

Type		two-seat escort and ground-attack fighter
Engine		Argus As-III 6-cylinder water-cooled inline, 180-hp
Armament		one fixed 7·92-mm Spandau machine gun and one flexible 7·92-mm Parabellum machine gun
Speed	103	mph at 16,400 feet
Climb	5	minutes 18 seconds to 3,280 feet
Ceiling	24,600	feet
Endurance	3	hours
Weight	1,577	lbs (empty)
	2,378	lbs (loaded)
Span	38	feet 4¾ inches
Length	24	feet 10½ inches
Height	9	feet 2¼ inches

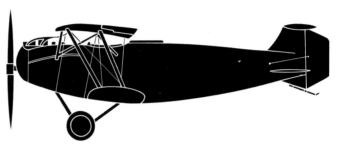

The Hannover CL-IIIa was one of Germany's best aircraft in World War I, and although it was a two-seater its manoeuvrability compared favourably with single-seaters'.

British Hawker Hart (1928)

Type		two-seat bomber
Engine		Rolls-Royce Kestrel 1B 12-cylinder liquid-cooled inline, 525-hp
Armament		one fixed ·303-inch Vickers gun and one flexible ·303-inch Lewis gun, plus up to 500 lbs of bombs
Speed	184	mph at 5,000 feet
Climb	8	minutes 20 seconds to 10,000 feet
Ceiling	21,000	feet
Range	470	miles
Weight	2,530	lbs (empty)
	4,554	lbs (loaded)
Span	37	feet 3 inches
Length	29	feet 4 inches
Height	10	feet 5 inches

The Hawker Hart was an extremely versatile two-seat biplane, originally designed as a light day bomber but subsequently adapted for several other roles. Nearly 1,000 were built, and many of these were exported.

British Handley Page Heyford (1930)

Type		four-seat heavy bomber
Engines		two Rolls-Royce Kestrel IIIS 12-cylinder liquid-cooled inlines, 575-hp each at 11,500 feet
Armament		three flexible ·303-inch Lewis guns and up to 3,500 lbs of bombs
Speed	142	mph at 12,500 feet
Ceiling	21,000	feet
Range	920	miles with 1,598-lb bomb-load
Weight	10,080	lbs (empty)
	16,750	lbs (loaded)
Span	75	feet
Length	58	feet
Height	20	feet 6 inches

The Handley Page Heyford was a very unusual machine: its fuselage was mounted under the top wing, the bomb-load was carried in the thickened centre section of the lower wing.

US Boeing P-26 (1932)

Type		single-seat fighter
Engine		Pratt & Whitney R-1340-27 9-cylinder air-cooled radial, 500-hp
Armament		two fixed ·3-inch or one ·3-inch and one ·5-inch machine gun, plus up to 200 lbs of bombs
Speed	234	mph at 7,500 feet
Climb	2,360	feet per minute initially
Ceiling	27,400	feet
Range	360	miles
Weight	2,197	lbs (empty)
	2,955	lbs (loaded)
Span	27	feet 11½ inches
Length	23	feet 7¼ inches
Height	10	feet 0½ inch

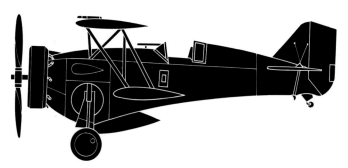

The Boeing P-26, nicknamed the 'Peashooter', was the USAAC's first all-metal, low-wing monoplane fighter.

US Curtiss F11C Goshawk (1932)

Type		single-seat carrier fighter-bomber
Engine		Wright R-1820-04 9-cylinder air-cooled radial, 700-hp
Armament		two fixed ·3-inch Browning machine guns, plus up to 474 lbs of bombs
Speed	225	mph at 8,000 feet
Climb	2	minutes 36 seconds to 5,000 feet
Ceiling	27,000	feet
Range	797	miles
Weight	3,329	lbs (empty)
	5,086	lbs (loaded)
Span	31	feet 6 inches
Length	23	feet
Height	10	feet 10 inches

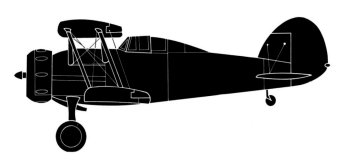

The Curtiss F11C, a versatile US Navy bomber-fighter, was chiefly remarkable for being a biplane with a retractable undercarriage.

British Gloster Gladiator (1934)

Type		single-seat fighter
Engine		Bristol Mercury IXS 9-cylinder air-cooled radial, 840-hp
Armament		four fixed ·303-inch Browning guns
Speed	253	mph at 14,500 feet
Climb	4	minutes 40 seconds to 10,000 feet
Ceiling	33,000	feet
Range	428	miles
Weight	3,217	lbs (empty)
	4,592	lbs (loaded)
Span	32	feet 3 inches
Length	27	feet 5 inches
Height	11	feet 9 inches

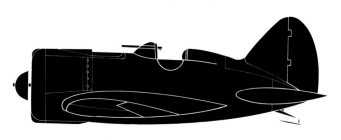

The Gloster Gladiator was the last biplane fighter to serve with British forces.

Russian Polikarpov I-16 (1934)

Type		single-seat fighter-bomber
Engine		Shvetsov M-62 9-cylinder air-cooled radial, 1,000-hp
Armament		two 20-mm ShVAK cannon, two 7·62-mm ShKAS machine guns, plus six 82-mm RS-82 rockets or two VAP-6M or ZAP-6 chemical containers
Speed	326	mph at sea level
Climb	4	minutes 48 seconds to 16,400 feet
Ceiling	29,530	feet
Range	435	miles
Weight	3,285	lbs (empty)
	4,520	lbs (loaded)
Span	29	feet 6½ inches
Length	20	feet 1¼ inches
Height	8	feet 5 inches

The Polikarpov I-16 was the first all-metal, low-wing, cantilever monoplane fighter in the world to be fitted with a retractable undercarriage, and performed sterling service with the Russian and Spanish Republican air forces before being relegated to training duties in the early months of 1943.

US Boeing B-17 Flying Fortress (1935)

Type		nine-seat heavy bomber
Engines		four Wright GR-1820-39 9-cylinder air-cooled radials, 930-hp each
Armament		five flexible ·3-inch Browning machine guns, plus up to 10,496 lbs of bombs
Speed	292	mph at 25,000 feet
Climb	6	minutes 30 seconds to 10,000 feet
Ceiling	36,000	feet
Range	2,400	miles
Weight	25,500	lbs (empty)
	47,920	lbs (loaded)
Span	103	feet 9 inches
Length	67	feet 11 inches
Height	15	feet 5 inches

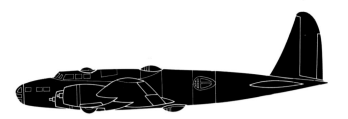

The Boeing B-17 was the United States' most celebrated bomber of World War II, and bore the brunt of the daylight offensive waged against Germany. The final mark, the 17G, differed quite considerably from the earlier prewar models, being very much better armed, and far less liable to catch fire when hit, the besetting problem of the first marks.

British Hawker Hurricane (1935)

Type		single-seat fighter-bomber
Engine		Rolls-Royce Merlin XX 12-cylinder liquid-cooled inline, 1,460-hp at take-off
Armament		four 20-mm Oerlikon cannon and up to 1,000 lbs of bombs
Speed	342	mph at 22,000 feet
Climb	9	minutes 6 seconds to 20,000 feet
Ceiling	35,600	feet
Range	970	miles
Weight	5,800	lbs (empty)
	7,800	lbs (loaded)
Span	40	feet
Length	32	feet 2½ inches
Height	8	feet 9 inches

The Hawker Hurricane was the first British fighter to be fitted with an armament of eight machine guns, and was the Spitfire's chief companion in the Battle of Britain. During this battle, Hurricanes shot down more German aircraft than all the other types combined. In its obsolescence it was transformed into an excellent fighter-bomber and tank-busting aircraft.

German Junkers Ju 87 (1935)

Type		two-seat dive-bomber and close support machine
Engine		Junkers Jumo 211J-1 12-cylinder liquid-cooled inline, 1,400-hp at take-off
Armament		two fixed 7·92-mm MG17 and one flexible 7·92-mm twin-barrelled MG8Iz machine gun, plus up to 3,968 lbs of bombs, or two pods containing six MG17 machine guns or two 2-cm MGFF cannon each, or two packs of 92 4·4-lb anti-personnel bombs
Speed	255	mph at 13,500 feet
Climb	19	minutes 48 seconds to 16,400 feet
Ceiling	23,905	feet
Range	954	miles
Weight	8,600	lbs (empty)
	14,550	lbs (loaded)
Span	45	feet 3⅓ inches
Length	37	feet 8¾ inches
Height	12	feet 9¼ inches

The Junkers Ju 87, more commonly known as the 'Stuka', was not an especially good machine, but performed very creditably in World War II with the aid of its devastating psychological impact.

German Messerschmitt Bf 109 (1935)

Type		single-seat fighter
Engine		Daimler-Benz 601E-1 12-cylinder liquid-cooled inline, 1,350-hp at take-off
Armament		one 2-cm MG151 cannon and two 7·92-mm MG17 machine guns
Speed	388	mph at 21,325 feet
Climb	2	minutes 36 seconds to 9,840 feet
Ceiling	39,370	feet
Range	528	miles
Weight	5,269	lbs (empty)
	6,872	lbs (loaded)
Span	32	feet 5¾ inches
Length	29	feet 0⅓ inch
Height	8	feet 6 inches

The Messerschmitt Bf 109, Germany's most celebrated fighter of the World War II era, was tested in combat in Spain, and much of real value was learned there, as regards both the aircraft and the tactics that suited it. It was built in greater numbers than any other German machine, but the need for heavier armament and more engine power at the end of the war detracted greatly from the type's flying characteristics, which peaked in the F of 1942.

Italian Savoia-Marchetti 81 *Pipistrello* (1935)

Type		six-seat bomber and transport machine
Engines		three Piaggio P.IX RC 40 9-cylinder air-cooled radials, 680-hp each
Armament		six flexible 7·7-mm machine guns and up to 2,205 lbs of bombs
Speed	205	mph at 13,120 feet
Ceiling	22,965	feet
Range	932	miles
Weight	14,300	lbs (empty)
	22,220	lbs (loaded)
Span	78	feet 8¾ inches
Length	58	feet 4¾ inches
Height	14	feet 7¼ inches

The Savoia-Marchetti 81 was for its time an excellent medium bomber, and proved very useful to the Italians in the conquest of Abyssinia and in the Spanish Civil War. The type was derived from a civilian airliner, and had a good performance coupled with a strong defensive armament of six machine guns. The *Pipistrello* (Bat) was obsolescent by World War II.

German Junkers Ju 88 (1936)

Type		three-seat bomber
Engines		two BMW 801G-2 14-cylinder air-cooled radials, 1,730-hp each at 5,000 feet
Armament		one flexible 13-mm MG131 machine gun, plus up to 4,410 lbs of bombs
Speed	340	mph at 26,250 feet
Ceiling	38,000	feet
Range	1,660	miles
Weight	18,250	lbs (empty)
	30,400	lbs (loaded)
Span	65	feet 7½ inches
Length	48	feet 2⅔ inches
Height	15	feet 8½ inches

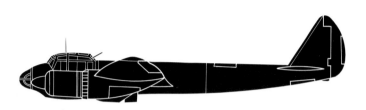

The Junkers Ju 88 was the most versatile aircraft produced by Germany in World War II, serving as a bomber, fighter, ground-attack, reconnaissance, anti-shipping, and night fighter. It was even pressed into service as the main component of a 'piggy-back' assault weapon, the nose being replaced by a large shaped charge.

British Short Sunderland (1937)

Type		13-seat maritime patrol and reconnaissance machine
Engines		four Pratt & Whitney R-1830-90B 14-cylinder air-cooled radials, 1,200-hp each
Armament		two ·5-inch and between eight and twelve ·303-inch Browning machine guns, plus up to 2,000 lbs of bombs
Speed	213	mph at 5,000 feet
Climb	840	feet per minute initially
Ceiling	17,600	feet
Range	2,980	miles
Weight	37,000	lbs (empty)
	60,000	lbs (loaded)
Span	112	feet 9½ inches
Length	85	fee 4 inches
Height	32	feet 10½ inches

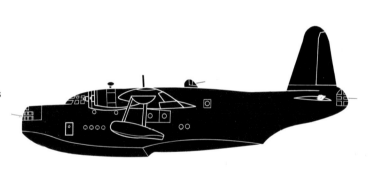

The Short Sunderland was designed to replace Britain's biplane patrol flying boats, and proved a remarkably successful machine, effective against U-boats and German long-range fighters.

British Bristol Beaufighter (1939)

Type		two-seat anti-shipping strike fighter
Engines		two Bristol Hercules XVII 14-cylinder air-cooled radials, 1,770-hp each
Armament		four 20-mm Hispano cannon, six ·303-inch Browning machine guns, one ·303-inch Vickers K gun, plus one 1,650-lb or 2,127-lb torpedo, or eight 90-lb rockets and two 250-lb bombs
Speed	303	mph at 1,300 feet
Ceiling	15,000	feet
Range	1,470	miles
Weight	15,600	lbs (empty)
	25,200	lbs (loaded)
Span	57	feet 10 inches
Length	41	feet 8 inches
Height	15	feet 10 inches

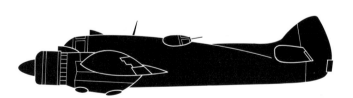

The Bristol Beaufighter was evolved from the Beaufort torpedo-bomber, but soon showed itself to be a far superior machine. It was a massive and sturdy machine, but possessed of considerable speed, range, and firepower. The Beaufighter was at its best as a heavily-armed, radar-equipped night fighter, or as an anti-shipping strike fighter with an armament of bombs, rockets, or an 18- or 21-inch torpedo.

Japanese Mitsubishi A6M *Zero-sen* (1939)

Type		single-seat carrier fighter
Engine		Nakajima NK1F Sakae 21 14-cylinder air-cooled radial, 1,130-hp at take-off
Armament		two 20-mm Type 99 cannon and two 7·7-mm Type 97 machine guns
Speed	338	mph at 19,685 feet
Climb	7	minutes 19 seconds to 19,685 feet
Ceiling	36,250	feet
Range	1,477	miles
Weight	3,984	lbs (empty)
	5,609	lbs (loaded)
Span	36	feet 1 inch
Length	29	feet 8¾ inches
Height	11	feet 6 inches

The Mitsubishi A6M, most commonly known as the Zero, was a landmark in naval fighter design, as it was the first such aircraft to be able to best its land-based counterparts. The capabilities of the Zero came as a rude shock to the Allies at the beginning of the Pacific war, and it was not until 1943 that a satisfactory counter was introduced. The Zero had excellent manoeuvrability and range, but lacked strength against heavy battle damage.

British de Havilland Mosquito (1940)

Type		two-seater bomber
Engines		two Rolls-Royce Merlin 21 12-cylinder liquid-cooled inlines, 1,460-hp each at 6,250 feet
Armament		up to 4,000 lbs of bombs
Speed	385	mph at 13,000 feet
Climb	2,500	feet per minute initially
Ceiling	34,000	feet
Range	2,040	miles
Weight	13,400	lbs (empty)
	22,570	lbs (loaded)
Span	54	feet 2 inches
Length	40	feet 9½ inches
Height	17	feet 5 inches

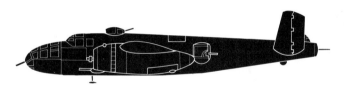

The de Havilland Mosquito was the British equivalent of the Junkers 88, and was first conceived as a bomber with speed sufficient to enable it to outrun German fighters, thus obviating the need for defensive armament. Performance was so spectacular, however, that the Mosquito was soon adapted as a fighter, night fighter, fighter bomber, reconnaissance machine, and anti-shipping strike fighter.

US North American B-25 Mitchell (1940)

Type		six-seat bomber
Engines		two Wright R-2600-92 14-cylinder air-cooled radials, 1,700-hp each
Armament		twelve ·5-inch Browning machine guns, plus eight 5-inch rockets and up to 3,000 lbs of bombs
Speed	272	mph at 12,000 feet
Ceiling	24,200	feet
Range	1,350	miles
Weight	19,480	lbs (empty)
	35,000	lbs (loaded)
Span	67	feet 7 inches
Length	52	feet 11 inches
Height	16	feet 4 inches

The North American Mitchell was one of the most important aircraft in the inventories of the Allies, being used by Russia, Britain, Holland, Brazil, and Canada as well as the United States. The B-25G and H models were exceptionally heavily armed ground-attack variants, being armed with a 75-mm gun in addition to 14 .5-inch machine guns, plus a torpedo or 3,200 lbs of bombs. The last model, the 25J, reverted to the conventional bomber design.

US North American P-51 Mustang (1940)

Type		single-seat escort fighter and fighter-bomber
Engine		Packard V-1650-7 Merlin 12-cylinder liquid-cooled inline, 1,694-hp
Armament		six ·5-inch Browning MG 53-2 machine guns, plus 2,000 lbs of bombs or six 5-inch rockets
Speed	437	mph at 25,000 feet
Climb	7	minutes 18 seconds to 20,000 feet
Ceiling	41,900	feet
Range	2,080	miles
Weight	7,125	lbs (empty)
	12,100	lbs (loaded)
Span	37	feet 0¼ inch
Length	32	feet 3 inches
Height	8	feet 8 inches

The North American Mustang, designed to a British specification, was undoubtedly the best fighter of World War II. The first mark, powered by an American Allison inline, performed creditably at low altitudes, but the marriage of the P-51 to the British Rolls-Royce Merlin in the P-51B paved the way for the development of the Mustang's remarkable abilities as a fighter and fighter-bomber.

US Vought F4U Corsair (1940)

Type		single-seat carrier fighter
Engine		Pratt & Whitney R-2800-8W 18-cylinder air-cooled radial, 2,250-hp
Armament		six ·5-inch Browning MG 53-2 machine guns, plus 2,000 lbs of bombs or eight 5-inch rockets
Speed	425	mph at 20,000 feet
Climb	3,120	feet per minute initially
Ceiling	37,000	feet
Range	1,562	miles
Weight	8,694	lbs (empty)
	13,120	lbs (loaded)
Span	40	feet 11 inches
Length	33	feet 4 inches
Height	15	feet 1 inch

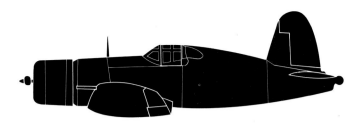

The Vought Corsair naval fighter and fighter-bomber was the best such machine of World War II, and proved to be an extremely potent machine, shooting down over 2,000 aircraft and providing fast, devastating support with guns, rockets, and bombs for US invasion forces in the Pacific theatre.

British Avro Lancaster (1941)

Type		seven-seat heavy bomber
Engines		four Rolls-Royce Merlin 24 12-cylinder liquid-cooled inlines, 1,640-hp each
Armament		ten flexible ·303-inch machine guns, plus up to 22,000 lbs of bombs
Speed	287	mph at 11,500 feet
Ceiling	24,500	feet
Range	1,660	miles
Weight	36,900	lbs (empty)
	70,000	lbs (loaded)
Span	102	feet
Length	69	feet 2 inches
Height	20	feet

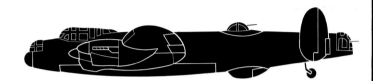

The Avro Lancaster was the best British bomber of World War II, and was a four-engined derivative of the ill-starred two-engined Manchester of 1939. Special adaptation enabled the Lancaster to carry the 22,000-lb 'Grand Slam', the largest bomb of the war, and another modification allowed the cylindrical 'dambuster' bomb to be used. The Lancaster was a sturdy and efficient machine, and bore the brunt of Bomber Command's night offensive against Germany.

US Grumman TBF Avenger (1941)

Type		three-seat carrier torpedo-bomber
Engine		Wright R-2600-8 14-cylinder air-cooled radial, 1,700-hp
Armament		one fixed ·3-inch, one flexible ·3-inch and one flexible ·5-inch Browning machine gun, plus 1,600 lbs of bombs or one 21-inch torpedo
Speed	271	mph at 12,000 feet
Climb	1,430	feet per minute initially
Ceiling	22,400	feet
Range	1,215	miles
Weight	10,080	lbs (empty)
	15,905	lbs (loaded)
Span	54	feet 2 inches
Length	40	feet
Height	16	feet 5 inches

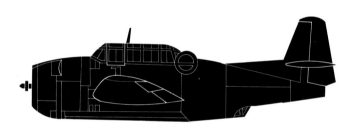

The Grumman Avenger was the US Navy's best torpedo-bomber of World War II, and was also able to pack a heavy punch with bombs and rockets. Nearly 1,000 of these versatile machines were supplied to the British Fleet Air Arm, with which they also had a distinguished career.

US Republic P-47 Thunderbolt (1941)

Type		single-seat escort fighter
Engine		Pratt & Whitney R-2800-59 18-cylinder air-cooled radial, 2,300-hp
Armament		eight ·5-inch Browning machine guns
Speed	433	mph at 30,000 feet
Climb	7	minutes 12 seconds to 15,000 feet
Ceiling	42,000	feet
Range	1,250	miles
Weight	9,900	lbs (empty)
	14,925	lbs (loaded)
Span	40	feet 9¾ inches
Length	35	feet 3¼ inches
Height	14	feet 1¾ inches

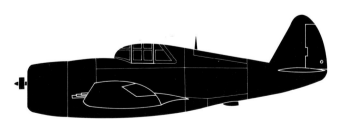

The magnificent Republic Thunderbolt was at the time of its introduction the largest and heaviest single-seat fighter in the world, and with eight .5-inch machine guns was very heavily armed. The all-round vision bubble canopy was introduced on the 47D. The type was also a formidable fighter-bomber.

US Boeing B-29 Superfortress (1942)

Type		ten-seat heavy bomber
Engines		four Wright R-3350 18-cylinder air-cooled radials, 2,200-hp each
Armament		eleven flexible ·5-inch Browning machine guns, plus up to 20,000 lbs of bombs
Speed	358	mph at 25,000 feet
Climb	38	minutes to 20,000 feet
Ceiling	31,850	feet
Range	3,250	miles
Weight	70,140	lbs (empty)
	124,000	lbs (loaded)
Span	141	feet 3 inches
Length	99	feet
Height	29	feet 7 inches

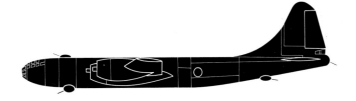

The Boeing Superfortress was designed to a USAAF requirement for a well-armed strategic bomber with excellent range. The design was exceptionally clean, with the engines closely cowled and conventional turrets, except that in the tail, replaced by remotely-controlled barbettes. With the elimination of Japanese air power, all defensive armament but the rear turret was often removed.

US Grumman F6F Hellcat (1942)

Type		single-seat carrier fighter and fighter-bomber
Engine		Pratt & Whitney R-2800-10W 18-cylinder air-cooled radial, 2,000-hp
Armament		six ·5-inch Browning machine guns, plus up to 2,000 lbs of bombs or six 5-inch rockets
Speed	386	mph at 17,300 feet
Climb	3,410	feet per minute initially
Ceiling	37,300	feet
Range	1,530	miles
Weight	9,153	lbs (empty)
	15,413	lbs (loaded)
Span	42	feet 10 inches
Length	33	feet 7 inches
Height	13	feet 1 inch

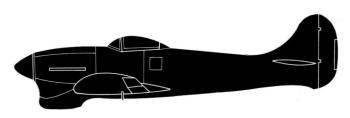

The Grumman Hellcat was a tubby naval fighter derived from the F4F Wildcat, and when it entered service in 1943, proved to be the first US aircraft in the Pacific capable of operating against the redoubtable Zero on anything like equal terms. Later models featured wing-mounted radar for night fighting, or provision for bombs or rockets for the fighter-bomber role. A further derivative, the F8F Bearcat, was about to enter service when war ended.

British Hawker Tempest (1942)

Type		single-seat fighter and fighter-bomber
Engine		Napier Sabre IIC 24-cylinder liquid-cooled inline, 2,180-hp
Armament		four 20-mm Hispano MK V cannon, plus 2,000 lbs of bombs or eight 60-lb rockets
Speed	426	mph at 18,500 feet
Climb	5	minutes to 15,000 feet
Ceiling	36,500	feet
Range	1,530	miles
Weight	9,000	lbs (empty)
	13,540	lbs (loaded)
Span	41	feet
Length	33	feet 8 inches
Height	16	feet 1 inch

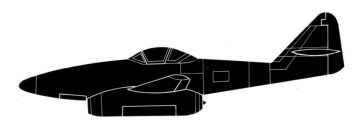

The Hawker Tempest, the culmination of Britain's land-based piston engined fighters, was built in two major marks: the Mark V with an inline engine, and the Mark II with a radial engine. The latter was too late to see wartime service. The Tempest V performed very ably in both the interceptor and ground-attack roles, in the latter proving a worthy successor to the Typhoon.

German Messerschmitt Me 262 (1942)

Type		single-seat fighter
Engines		two Junkers Jumo 004B-1 turbojets, 1,980-lbs static thrust each
Armament		four 3-cm MK108 cannon
Speed	540	mph at 19,685 feet
Climb	6	minutes 48 seconds to 19,685 feet
Ceiling	37,565	feet
Range	652	miles
Weight	8,378	lbs (empty)
	14,101	lbs (loaded)
Span	40	feet 11½ inches
Length	34	feet 9½ inches
Height	12	feet 7 inches

The Messerschmitt 262 was the world's first jet-powered operational fighter, and marked the beginning of a new era in fighter design. Although the Allies produced jet fighters of their own, they were essentially piston-engined in concept, while the swept wings of the Me 262 showed the true road ahead.

Russian Lavochkin La-7 (1943)

Type		single-seat fighter and fighter-bomber
Engine		Shvetsov ASh-82FNU 14-cylinder air-cooled radial, 1,775-hp
Armament		three 20-mm ShVAK cannon, plus up to 330 lbs of bombs
Speed	425	mph at 18,372 feet
Climb	4	minutes 27 seconds to 16,400 feet
Ceiling	34,448	feet
Range	394	miles
Weight	?	(empty)
	7,495	lbs (loaded)
Span	32	feet 2 inches
Length	27	feet 10½ inches
Height	9	feet 3 inches

The Lavochkin 7 exemplified all the salient features of Russian fighter design: careful development from earlier models (in this case the La-5), simple but clean aerodynamics, a powerful engine, good armament, and lack of unnecessary sophistication. This last meant that serviceability was high, and maintenance simple on the poor airfields the Russians had to use. Moreover, Russian fighters were the equal of most German and Allied machines.

Russian Mikoyan-Gurevich MiG-15 (1947)

Type		single-seat fighter
Engine		VK-1A turbojet, 6,990-lbs thrust with water injection
Armament		one 30-mm N and two 23-mm NS cannon, plus up to 1,100 lbs of bombs or rockets
Speed	746	mph at 10,000 feet
Climb	10,400	feet per minute initially
Ceiling	51,000	feet
Range	560	miles
Weight	11,085	lbs (loaded)
Span	33	feet 1 inch
Length	36	feet 3¼ inches
Height	11	feet 1¾ inches

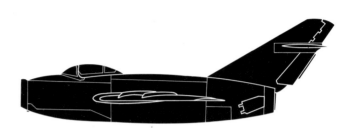

The MiG-15 was the Sabre's best opponent over Korea, and served in great numbers both with the Red Air Force and with the air forces of the Russian satellites. It had a better rate of climb and ceiling than the Sabre, as well as a tighter turn and superior speed.

US North American F-86 Sabre (1947)

Type		single-seat fighter and fighter-bomber
Engine		General Electric J47-GE-13 turbojet, 5,200-lbs static thrust
Armament		six ·5-inch Browning machine guns, plus 2,000 lbs of bombs or sixteen 5-inch rockets
Speed	675	mph at 2,500 feet
Climb	7,630	feet per minute initially
Ceiling	48,300	feet
Range	785	miles
Weight	10,495	lbs (empty)
	16,357	lbs (loaded)
Span	37	feet 1 inch
Length	37	feet 6 inches
Height	14	feet 8 inches

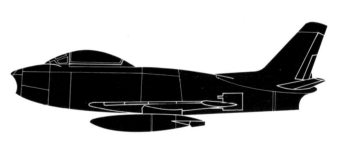

The North American Sabre was a classic postwar first-generation jet fighter, and proved its worth in the air over Korea in the early 1950s. By European and Russian standards, however, it was lacking in weight of armament, having only machine guns instead of cannon.

British English Electric Canberra (1949)

Type		two-seater night interdictor or high-altitude bomber
Engines		two Rolls-Royce Avon Mark 109 turbojets, 7,400-lbs static thrust each
Armament		four 20-mm Hispano cannon and 3,000 lbs of bombs, or 6,000 lbs of bombs
Speed	541	mph at 40,000 feet
Ceiling	48,000	feet
Range	3,630	miles
Weight	56,250	lbs (loaded)
Span	63	feet 11½ inches
Length	65	feet 6 inches
Height	15	feet 8 inches
Climb	3,800	feet per minute initially

The English Electric Canberra was the first jet bomber to serve with the Royal Air Force, established several world records, and was the only British aircraft to have been built under licence in the United States since World War II until the Harrier. Many have also been exported to countries all over the world. The Canberra is a very clean design and has excellent manoeuvrability, sufficient to warrant one version, the B(I) Mark 8 and its derivatives, being fitted with a cannon armament for use in the interdiction role.

British Hawker Hunter (1951)

Type		single-seat fighter and ground attack aircraft
Engine		Rolls-Royce Avon Mk 203 turbojet, 10,000-lbs static thrust
Armament		four 30-mm Aden cannon, plus up to 2,000 lbs of bombs and various combinations of rockets
Speed	Mach 0·95	at 36,000 feet
Climb	7	minutes 30 seconds to 45,000 feet
Ceiling	51,500	feet
Range	1,650	miles
Weight	12,760	lbs (empty)
	24,000	lbs (loaded)
Span	33	feet 8 inches
Length	45	feet 10½ inches
Height	13	feet 2 inches

The Hawker Hunter was one of the classic jet aircraft designed after World War II, and proved the most successful subsonic jet fighter exported by Great Britain—over 400 in all, with another 460 built under licence. Early marks were intended as pure fighters, but later marks, developed as the basic design began to grow obsolescent, had dual capabilities as fighters and ground-attack machines.

US Lockheed F-104 Starfighter (1954)

Type		single-seat fighter-bomber
Engine		General Electric J79-GE-7 turbojet, 10,000-lbs static thrust (15,800-lbs with afterburning)
Armament		one 20-mm six-barrel Vulcan cannon, plus 2,000 lbs of bombs or two or four Sidewinder air-to-air missiles
Speed	1,450	mph at 40,000 feet
Climb	40,000	feet per minute initially
Ceiling	55,000+	feet
Range	1,000+	miles
Weight	14,300	lbs (empty)
	23,590	lbs (loaded)
Span	21	feet 11 inches
Length	54	feet 9 inches
Height	13	feet 6 inches

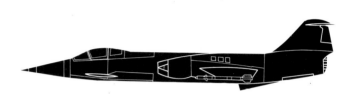

The Lockheed Starfighter was designed as a very high performance day interceptor fighter, and as such was built in limited numbers for use by the US Air Force. However, the design attracted much foreign interest, and the Starfighter has since been adapted to several other missions, the most important being ground-attack. Most of these later developments have been built under licence by manufacturers in Canada, Germany, Italy, Holland, Belgium, and Holland. It is also used by Pakistan, Turkey, Norway, and others.

Russian Mikoyan-Gurevich MiG-21 (1955)

Type		single-seat fighter
Engine		Tumansky RD-11 F300 turbojet, 13,000-lbs static thrust with afterburning
Armament		one 30-mm cannon, plus two K-13 AAMs or two pods with 16 55-mm rockets
Speed	Mach 2	at 45,000+ feet
Climb	30,000	feet per minute initially
Ceiling	65,000+	feet
Range	700	miles
Weight	12,100	lbs (empty)
	17,000	lbs (loaded)
Span	23	feet 5½ inches
Length	51	feet 8½ inches (including nose boom)
Height	14	feet 9 inches

The MiG-21 has been the standard fighter of the Soviet Union, its satellites, and allies throughout the 1960s and early 1970s, and is built under licence in Czechoslovakia and India. Main armament consists of two cannon and two air-to-air missiles, but other stores can be carried on a pylon under the fuselage. Several improved versions of the basic design have been produced, as well as an experimental STOL version with lift engines in the fuselage. It is supplemented at present by the Mach 3 MiG-23 fighter.

French Dassault Mirage III (1956)

Type		single-seat fighter and ground attack aircraft
Engine		SNECMA Atar 09B3 turbojet, 13,225-lbs static thrust with afterburning, plus optional SEPR 844 rocket, 3,700 lbs thrust
Armament		two 30-mm DEFA cannon, plus up to 4,000 lbs of bombs or Matra R.511 or 530 AAMs, Sidewinder AAMs, or Nord AS.30 air-to-ground missiles
Speed	Mach 2·15	at 50,000 feet
Climb	30,000+	feet per minute initially
Ceiling	65,000+	feet
Range	1,500	miles
Weight	?	(empty)
	26,015	lbs (loaded)
Span	27	feet
Length	48	feet 5½ inches
Height	13	feet 11½ inches

The Dassault Mirage III has been one of the most successful aircraft since World War II, and has been operated in combat with considerable success by the Israeli air force. It is also in service with the air forces of several other countries.

2: Rate of Aircraft Development 1903-74

As has been pointed out by Robin Higham in his admirable *Air Power: a concise history*, the representation of the development of military aircraft in diagrammatic form reveals two very interesting factors, complementary but in certain ways entirely independent of each other.

The first of these factors is concerned with the influence of war. Before the outbreak of war, growth or decline are usually quite steady, but as the imminence of war becomes apparent, there is a sharp rise in the effort devoted to aircraft development, this leading to a period of instability about the time that war breaks out; once the war is into its stride, and war production is under way, there is a spectacular (but steady) increase in effort until the end, or realization of the approach of the end, of the war. There then follows a period of unsettled decline as the war effort is tapered off. In World War I this decline caught the aircraft industry at a very poor time. For in 1918 the fruits of four years work in structures, engines, and aerodynamics were about to result in a crop of advanced designs; these were now abandoned, and aviation in general took a severe knock. In World War II, Allied aircraft design reached a peak in 1944 with the ultimate piston-engined aircraft. Only Germany from this time onwards was still making progress – she had to in order to stave off the approaching Allied victory. The Allies, realising that victory was in their pockets, could afford to relax their efforts. A similar pattern (on a smaller scale) is discernible in the various conflicts and ups or downs in the 'cold war' since 1945.

The second factor apparent in the diagram reflects on the whole of the development of military aircraft in the last three-quarters of a century. This factor is the gradual growth upwards of the line of development. Robin Higham likens this to the development of a person from infancy to middle age. Unfortunately, this leads one to suppose that there will be an old age and senility in the development of aircraft, which will not (hopefully) be the case. It would perhaps be better to avoid analogies of this nature, but merely point out that there is a general upward trend despite the major upheavals caused by wars.

With reference to the diagram, it should be noted that this is only meant to give a relative indication of the growth of the art: the fact that the line is twice as high at one point than at another should not be taken to mean that twice as much effort was expended at the second point compared with the first. It should also be noted that at times the state of the art may be high, but that the effort is negated by factors outside the aviation industry: an example of this can be found in the cancellation of the TSR-2 project and similar occurrences when the state of the art, *in se*, was at a high level.

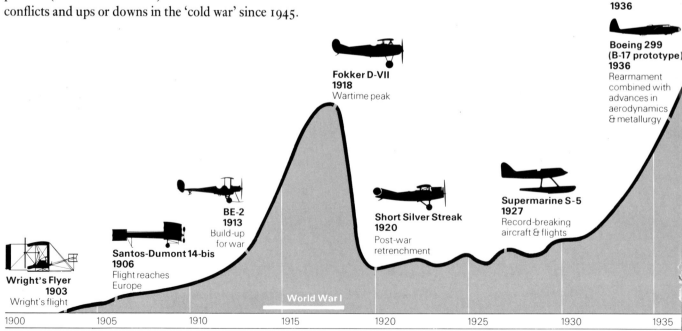

Hawker Hurrica
1936

Boeing 299
(B-17 prototype)
1936
Rearmament combined with advances in aerodynamics & metallurgy

Fokker D-VII
1918
Wartime peak

BE-2
1913
Build-up for war

Supermarine S-5
1927
Record-breaking aircraft & flights

Short Silver Streak
1920
Post-war retrenchment

Santos-Dumont 14-bis
1906
Flight reaches Europe

Wright's Flyer
1903
Wright's flight

World War I

1900   1905   1910   1915   1920   1925   1930   1935

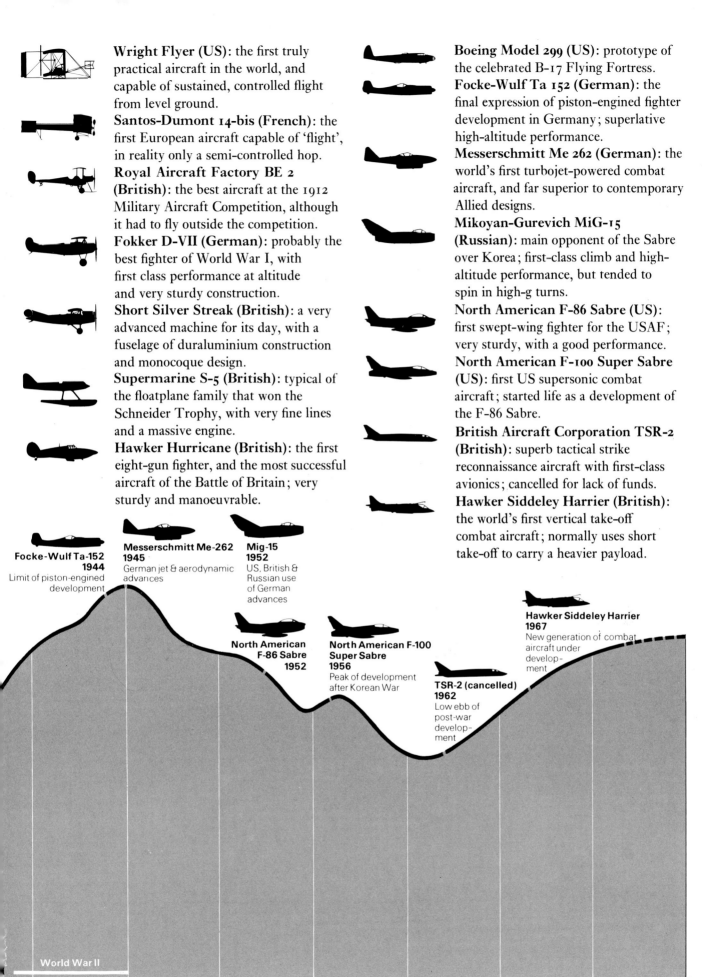

Wright Flyer (US): the first truly practical aircraft in the world, and capable of sustained, controlled flight from level ground.

Santos-Dumont 14-bis (French): the first European aircraft capable of 'flight', in reality only a semi-controlled hop.

Royal Aircraft Factory BE 2 (British): the best aircraft at the 1912 Military Aircraft Competition, although it had to fly outside the competition.

Fokker D-VII (German): probably the best fighter of World War I, with first class performance at altitude and very sturdy construction.

Short Silver Streak (British): a very advanced machine for its day, with a fuselage of duraluminium construction and monocoque design.

Supermarine S-5 (British): typical of the floatplane family that won the Schneider Trophy, with very fine lines and a massive engine.

Hawker Hurricane (British): the first eight-gun fighter, and the most successful aircraft of the Battle of Britain; very sturdy and manoeuvrable.

Boeing Model 299 (US): prototype of the celebrated B-17 Flying Fortress.

Focke-Wulf Ta 152 (German): the final expression of piston-engined fighter development in Germany; superlative high-altitude performance.

Messerschmitt Me 262 (German): the world's first turbojet-powered combat aircraft, and far superior to contemporary Allied designs.

Mikoyan-Gurevich MiG-15 (Russian): main opponent of the Sabre over Korea; first-class climb and high-altitude performance, but tended to spin in high-g turns.

North American F-86 Sabre (US): first swept-wing fighter for the USAF; very sturdy, with a good performance.

North American F-100 Super Sabre (US): first US supersonic combat aircraft; started life as a development of the F-86 Sabre.

British Aircraft Corporation TSR-2 (British): superb tactical strike reconnaissance aircraft with first-class avionics; cancelled for lack of funds.

Hawker Siddeley Harrier (British): the world's first vertical take-off combat aircraft; normally uses short take-off to carry a heavier payload.

Focke-Wulf Ta-152 1944
Limit of piston-engined development

Messerschmitt Me-262 1945
German jet & aerodynamic advances

Mig-15 1952
US, British & Russian use of German advances

North American F-86 Sabre 1952

North American F-100 Super Sabre 1956
Peak of development after Korean War

TSR-2 (cancelled) 1962
Low ebb of post-war development

Hawker Siddeley Harrier 1967
New generation of combat aircraft under development

World War II

1940 1945 1950 1955 1960 1965 1970 1975

ABOVE *Two Royal Navy Vixens refuel as they pass overhead.*